Also by david nolman

The Art Of Alignment :Crafting your Inner and Outer Mastery

Echoes of Eternity

Unlocking Thoth's Ancient Mysteries

by

David Holman

Echoes of Eternity: Unlocking Thoth's Ancient Mysteries

Contents

Chapter 11: Unlocking the Secrets: Interpretative Challenges

Diverse Interpretations Over Time

Personal Reflection and Understanding

Chapter 12: Renewing the Quest for Ancient Wisdom

Thoth's Role in the Quest for Knowledge Today

The Continuing Influence on Personal Growth

Conclusion

Appendix A: Appendix

Additional Resources for Further Study

Glossary of Key Terms and Concepts

Introduction

The Emerald Tablets have long been shrouded in mystery, capturing the imagination of seekers, scholars, and mystics throughout history. Cloaked in the allure of ancient wisdom and esoteric knowledge, these cryptic texts are believed to contain the secrets of the universe as relayed by the enigmatic figure of Thoth, the ancient Egyptian god of wisdom, writing, and magic. The allure of the Tablets is not just in their antiquity but in the profound insights they are believed to offer—a blueprint for spiritual ascension, alchemical transformation, and universal truths. But what is it about these ancient writings that have allowed them to endure across millennia, inspiring countless individuals and influencing a multitude of spiritual and philosophical traditions?

The journey into understanding the Emerald Tablets begins with an appreciation for the time and culture in which they emerged. It is said that the Tablets were composed by Thoth himself, also known as Hermes Trismegistus in Greco-Roman traditions, a figure of not just historical but mythological importance. His wisdom, encoded in the Tablets, is thought to transcend the boundaries of time and place, acting as a conduit between the physical and the metaphysical. This lends an air of divinity and mystery to the Tablets, drawing those in search of hidden truths. The stories surrounding their origin evoke a sense of wonder, hinting at lost civilizations and forgotten knowledge. However, beyond the mystery lies a clear goal—the unveiling of ancient wisdom to guide contemporary seekers on their path to enlightenment.

The resonance of the Emerald Tablets extends far beyond their historical roots in Egypt. As one delves into their intricacies, it's not just the content that captivates but the universal nature of the messages they carry. They speak of unity, the interconnectedness of all things, and the balance of opposites—concepts that are cornerstone tenets of various spiritual practices today. So, how do these ancient symbols and teachings integrate into modern life? The answer lies in their adaptability. The Tablets have served as fertile grounds for the emergence of Hermeticism, a tradition that has permeated numerous cultural expressions and continues to wield influence in the realms of alchemy, esoteric philosophy, and even psychology.

Yet the Tablets are not only a relic of the past; they are a living document, flexible in interpretation and vast in scope. Across the ages, scholars and mystics have pondered over their meanings, offering interpretations that align with the shifting paradigms of their times. In today's world, laden with uncertainty and a thirst for deeper understanding, the teachings of the Emerald Tablets hold a unique appeal. They provide a framework for those seeking purpose, offering insights into the nature of reality and consciousness. Their continuing impact cannot be overstated, with modern thinkers drawing parallels between their teachings and the principles of modern physics and metaphysical philosophies.

This book aims to embark on a comprehensive exploration of the Emerald Tablets, unpacking their mythological origins and tracing their journey from legend to artifact. By delving into the symbolic language and metaphors that weave the fabric of the Tablets, we gain insights into the mind of Thoth and the essence of the wisdom he sought to impart. We will investigate not only the esoteric aspects but also the tangible influence these writings have had in shaping spiritual thought across cultures and epochs. Through a blend of narrative, description, and inspiration, this book intends to offer a doorway to ancient wisdom, inviting you to integrate these age-old teachings into modern life.

The relevance of the Tablets today is undeniable. As humanity stands on the cusp of unprecedented change and discovery, the inner truths encapsulated in these writings offer guidance. Contemporary spirituality often borrows from these ancient teachings, channeling their insights into new frameworks and interpretations that speak to the soul's eternal quest for knowledge. By exploring the Tablets, we can engage in a dialogue with the past, allowing us to rediscover profound insights that hold the potential to transform both individual lives and collective consciousness.

In this quest to unveil ancient wisdom, we will examine Thoth's enduring legacy, the archaeological discoveries that have brought the Tablets to light, and the deep philosophical underpinnings of their teachings. Each chapter will build upon the last, painting a holistic picture that traverses cultures, time periods, and spiritual practices. This exploration is both an academic inquiry and a personal journey, inviting reflection and introspection as we seek understanding within. In this way, the Emerald Tablets continue to fulfill their divine purpose, serving as a beacon of light for all who seek to understand the deeper layers of existence, hoping to decipher the mysteries that lie within.

Chapter 1: The Mythical Origins of the Emerald Tablets

The tale of the Emerald Tablets is one that dances between the realms of myth and reality. Veiled in mystery, these ancient relics are said to contain the wisdom of Thoth, the enigmatic figure revered as the god of wisdom and writing in ancient Egypt. Legends tell of how Thoth, known for his incomprehensible intellect, inscribed the tablets at the dawn of time, imbuing them with secrets of the cosmos and alchemical transformations. But where do these stories begin, and how have they shaped our understanding of this mystical legacy?

Thoth occupies a central role in Egyptian mythology, depicted as the ibis-headed scribe of the gods. It is said that his revelations guided the creation of the very laws that governed the universe. As the supposed author of these tablets, Thoth's influence on Egyptian culture was monumental, transcending time and space. His knowledge was believed to bridge the corporeal and the divine, offering insights into the workings of the universe that few could fathom. This connection to the divine fueled the multitude of stories surrounding the origins of the Emerald Tablets.

Stories and myths feed on the fascination with the unknown, and the Emerald Tablets are no exception. From the peripheries of history, these tablets have captivated the minds of seekers, scholars, and mystics alike. Many believe these tablets were hidden away, scattered across distant lands, or even spirited to the astral realm. Each legend and tale adds another layer of allure and mystery, tempting the curious to delve into their secrets and ponder their origins.

The mythology surrounding the Emerald Tablets is a testament to humanity's quest for knowledge and understanding. These narratives invite us to question the boundaries of what we know and inspire the enduring search for hidden truths. In the search, we might just find a glimpse of the wisdom that has eluded so many across the ages.

Understanding Thoth's Legacy

Embedded in the heart of ancient Egyptian mythology is the enigmatic figure of Thoth, a deity whose legacy is intricately connected to the mystical Emerald Tablets. Revered as the god of wisdom, writing, and knowledge, Thoth's contributions go beyond mere myth. His teachings offer a window into the profound spiritual and intellectual pursuits of Egypt's ancients. While the details of the Emerald Tablets remain shrouded in mystery, to decipher Thoth's legacy is to embark on an exploration of esoteric wisdom that has influenced generations.

Thoth, often depicted with the head of an ibis or a baboon, was not just a scribe of the gods; he was the architect of language and the keeper of divine records. In Egyptian tradition, Thoth is credited with the creation of hieroglyphics, the sacred script that allowed communication and documentation of spiritual and practical knowledge. His influence extended beyond writing and was believed to include the authoring of the very laws that governed both human and celestial realms. The mythological narratives cast him as a mediator in the battles of light and darkness, underscoring his role as a cosmic balance keeper.

The Emerald Tablets, attributed to Thoth, offer a cryptic collection of aphorisms that encapsulate universal truths. Despite their elusive origins, these texts are said to contain the secrets of alchemy and the transmutation of the soul, exploring themes of cosmic order and the fundamental principles of life. Legend has it that the tablets were inscribed by Thoth himself, using an indestructible green pigment, symbolizing eternal wisdom. The quest to unravel these secrets has intrigued scholars, mystics, and seekers of knowledge for centuries, perpetuating Thoth's influence long after the decline of Egyptian civilization.

What distinguishes Thoth's legacy is its enduring impact. The conceptual frameworks emerging from his association with the

Emerald Tablets resonate with the philosophies of Hermeticism, which forms a significant junction between the ancient and the modern. From the concept of 'as above, so below' to the emphasis on transformation and unity with the divine, Hermetic ideas echo the teachings of Thoth, demonstrating their adaptability across time and cultures. Rather than static doctrines, these teachings present a dynamic spirituality, shaping personal and collective destinies through mystical and practical application.

Thoth's legacy, filtered through the Emerald Tablets, reveals a vision of the universe as an interconnected whole, where understanding higher truths could lead to enlightenment. This vision appeals to modern seekers who grapple with the complexities of existence and the quest for personal growth. In today's fast-paced world, returning to these ancient teachings offers a pause for reflection and a source of philosophical depth, urging us to ponder the timeless questions of life, consciousness, and the cosmos.

In tracing Thoth's legacy, it's crucial to recognize that it isn't merely an academic exercise; it's an invitation to embrace wisdom that transcends epochs. His image as the archetypal wise guide continues to inspire those searching for meaning in a transient world. Whether through ritual practice, scholarly study, or contemplative meditation, engaging with Thoth's teachings offers a timeless blueprint for those aiming to balance intellectual inquiry with spiritual enlightenment.

The legacy of Thoth, as viewed through the Emerald Tablets, holds a mirror to humanity's perennial pursuit of knowledge. It challenges us to question, to seek, and ultimately, to understand the mysteries that lie at the intersection of myth and reality. As we peel back the layers of history, we uncover a clarity that speaks not just of the past, but of potential futures, allowing the legacy of Thoth to continue as a beacon of enlightened wisdom.

Thoth's Role in Ancient Egyptian Culture serves as a cornerstone in understanding the expansive legacy left by this enigmatic figure, revered for millennia as the architect of writing, wisdom, and the mystical arts. Thoth, often depicted as an ibis-headed deity, wielded influence that stretched far beyond mere scribal duties. His presence permeated the very essence of ancient Egyptian culture, embedding itself within the intricacies of their cosmology, religion, and daily life.

As the god credited with inventing the hieroglyphs, Thoth's contributions to Egyptian society were nothing short of revolutionary. He transformed the realm of communication, enabling the recording of events, religious texts, and royal decrees—artifacts that have survived the ravages of time to inform our understanding of these ancient beginnings. Thoth was believed to stand at cosmic crossroads, balancing the forces of order and chaos. The Egyptians saw in him not just a communicator of divine truths but a keeper of the cosmic ledger, tasked with maintaining the universe's equilibrium.

The mythological stories surrounding Thoth paint a rich tapestry of his roles and exploits. He featured prominently in the "Five Books of Thoth," a legendary narrative that the ancient scribes believed contained all the knowledge of the universe. Thoth's wisdom, as recorded in these mythical texts, offered pathways to immortality and the secrets of the heavens—a precious link to the divine realms. It's no wonder that Thoth became the patron of scribes and scholars, those seekers of wisdom who would carry forth his legacy through generations.

In religious rituals, Thoth occupied roles that were vital and multifaceted. He served as a mediator during the celestial proceedings of the afterlife, notably in the weighing of the heart ceremony, where his presence ensured that divine justice was meted out accurately. This positioned Thoth as both a judge and an advocate, ushering souls to their rightful places in the afterlife. Such roles amplified his image as a guardian of moral and ethical guidelines, an essential pillar for the Ma'at—the ancient Egyptian concept of truth, balance, and cosmic order.

Beyond religious texts and mythology, Thoth's influence extended to more practical domains—and one can't overlook his impact on scientific advancement and intellectual pursuits. He was venerated as the originator of scientific art forms, including astronomy, mathematics, medicine, and even magic, which the Egyptians did not entirely disentangle from other scientific fields. Thoth embodied a synergy between spiritual belief and empirical inquiry, blending the known world with the mysteries that lay beyond perception.

This god of wisdom was also intimately tied to the moon, an association that symbolized his role in measuring time. The cycles of the moon, with their dependable regularity, linked Thoth to lunar calendars and the rhythms of life in the agrarian society of Egypt. For the Egyptians, who relied heavily on the Nile's predictable floods for agriculture, Thoth's lunar connections would have reinforced his image as a provider of guidance and foreknowledge. Through these cycles, he taught the importance of timing and patience—virtues engrained in the responsibilities of farmers, priests, and healers.

Architecturally, the temples dedicated to Thoth stand as testament to his widespread influence. In regions such as Hermopolis, where his worship was particularly concentrated, temples became centers of learning and wisdom. These structures served as gathering points for sages and scholars who engaged in complex theological debates and experiments, channeling Thoth's legacy of knowledge. Such environments nurtured the philosophical underpinnings crucial to later Hellenistic interpretations of Thoth, as Hermes Trismegistus, and cemented his stature across disciplines and cultures.

Moreover, Thoth's significance persisted in art, where his images carried symbolic meanings interwoven with the quotidian and the divine. Artists captured his image on papyri, murals, and carvings, meticulously recording his tales and imparting his essence into the culture. The depiction of Thoth holding the ankh and scribe's palette was more than mere iconography; it was a visual enchiridion of knowledge and life, presented for all generations to come.

By intertwining Thoth with their spiritual and intellectual pursuits, the ancient Egyptians fostered a culture that revered learning as an act of devotion and a means of approaching the divine. Thoth's legacy in this milieu catalyzed a reverence for knowledge that transcended time and space, reverberating in philosophies and practices far removed from their original soil. Indeed, Thoth's role morphed and expanded, influencing not only his kin's understanding of wisdom and the cosmos but also leaving indelible marks on Hermeticism, modern metaphysical thought, and alchemy.

Thoth's enduring role in Egyptian society demonstrates more than a penchant for storytelling; it reveals a sophisticated integration of knowledge, spirituality, and everyday life. His dual role as keeper of sacred wisdom and chronicler of the eternal dance between chaos and order underscores the Egyptians' pursuit of balance in divinity and reality. As we continue to delve into the mythical origins of the Emerald Tablets, Thoth remains an eternal guide, whose ancient wisdom offers continuing illumination on our path towards deeper truths.

The Mythology Surrounding the Tablets

Steeped in the enigma of time, the Emerald Tablets carry tales wrapped in the cloaks of mythology and mysticism. Originating from a world where divine beings and mortals often intermingled, these tablets are said to have been created by Thoth, the ancient Egyptian deity of wisdom, writing, and knowledge. Tradition holds that Thoth inscribed these tablets with secrets so profound that they held the power to unlock the mysteries of the universe.

Imagining their provenance is akin to wandering through a mythical landscape where history and legend blur. As the god of wisdom, Thoth was not only a patron of scribes but also the keeper of arcane knowledge. The Emerald Tablets are believed to be his magnum opus, an opus that transcends time and space. Their origins trace a path through stories that describe Thoth descending from the heavens, bringing with him wisdom to enlighten mankind.

Embedded in this mythology is the notion that the tablets hold the keys to immortality and transformation. They weren't merely static pieces of text but living embodiments of Thoth's teachings and power. The mythos suggests that anyone who fully understood the inscriptions would unlock the ability to transcend mundane limitations, achieving both physical transformation and spiritual enlightenment.

For centuries, seekers have been fascinated by the divine provenance of these tablets. Some traditions claim that the Emerald Tablets were formed from a single piece of emerald that fell from Lucifer's crown when he was cast out of heaven. This embeds a celestial quality to their narrative, attributing them an origin both sinister and divine. Others speculate that the tablets were crafted in a lost civilization, a place of advanced knowledge and spiritual acumen, perhaps Atlantis itself. In this telling, the fall of Atlantis was not just a physical collapse but a spiritual fragmentation, with the tablets being a surviving relic of that glorious epoch.

The intrigue does not end with their creation. The journey of the tablets through history resembles an epic quest where many have sought, but few have truly comprehended their depths. Legends spun around these tablets speak of them being closely guarded by generations of mystics, alchemists, and philosophers, who understood their potential yet recognized the dangers of their powerful secrets falling into unscrupulous hands.

One of the more beguiling myths involves Alexander the Great. It is said that during his conquests, Alexander stumbled upon the fabled city of Alexandria, under which the Emerald Tablets were hidden. The story contends that Alexander's legendary insights and strategies were, in part, inspired by his secret readings of these mystical artifacts. While historians debate the veracity of such tales, they illustrate a vivid tapestry of myth that cannot be easily unraveled from the fabric of historical narrative.

In esoteric circles, the Emerald Tablets elevate Thoth from mere mythology to a symbol of eternal wisdom. They depict Thoth not only as an Egyptian god but as a timeless figure, transcending cultural and temporal boundaries. Ancient Greek philosophers identified him with Hermes, giving rise to the Hermetic tradition. Thus, the mythology surrounding the tablets also serves as a crucible where different belief systems merge, hinting at a universal wisdom accessible to those who truly seek it.

This intertwining of myth and reality doesn't just adorn the imagination—it inspires profound aspiration. The Emerald Tablets have, throughout history, ignited a quest for knowledge that transcends the limitations of tangible exploration. They embody a cosmic journey into the depths of the unknown, a journey that promises transformative enlightenment to those courageous and wise enough to undertake it.

The enduring allure of these tablets lies in their invocation of mystery and promise of revelation, perpetuating a cycle of curiosity and wonder. Aspiring scholars and modern mystics alike are compelled by the age-old question of what truths these emerald inscriptions might unveil. Invariably, the mythology of the Emerald Tablets serves as both a mirror reflecting humanity's eternal pursuit of knowledge and a labyrinth inviting the seeker to navigate its enigmatic pathways.

Chapter 2: Discovering the Tablets

As the mystical allure of the Emerald Tablets whispered through the ages, it was inevitable that scholars and mystics alike found themselves irresistibly drawn to their enigmatic origins. The journey to uncover these legendary artifacts was far from a straightforward path. In a world caught between myth and reality, many questioned whether the Tablets were merely a creation of the imagination or genuine relics of ancient wisdom.

Archaeological endeavors in the early 20th century marked the beginning of a deeper exploration into these whispers of old. These pursuits aimed to bridge the gap between lore and physical evidence. Significant excavations unfurled across Egypt, the land eternally intertwined with Thoth, the deity many credited with the creation of the Tablets. Each dig site echoed with the promise of discovery, as if the land itself had tales waiting to be told.

Among these excavations, a significant site emerged — a location steeped in mystery, where fragments hinting at the existence of the Tablets came to light. These discoveries were not just about artifacts; they spoke of a civilization where the cosmos, nature, and divine insight intertwined. The landscape bore silent witness to these revelations, as seekers unearthed objects and inscriptions that danced on the edge of the known and the unknown.

The journey of these discoveries didn't simply revolve around validation of the myth; it was also about the broader context of ancient cultures and their spiritual frameworks. As items surfaced, scholars and historians deduced that the Emerald Tablets were emblematic of an era where wisdom transcended mere human boundaries. The Tablets didn't belong to a temple or a tomb but appeared to exist in a metaphorical temple of the mind, accessible to those prepared to seek knowledge with an open spirit.

Yet, the path from legend to artifact was not without its skeptics. Many in academia questioned the authenticity of these finds, suggesting they might be elaborate hoaxes or misunderstood relics with unrelated origins. Despite these debates, the fascination surrounding the Tablets persisted, fueled by the notion that they contained truths from a time when man and the divine seemed inseparably connected.

As stories of these findings spread, the Tablets began to occupy a unique space in contemporary thought — symbols not of a lost past but of enduring significance. They prompted questions that transcended mere historical inquiry. What wisdom could be gleaned from such texts? How did these ancient symbols speak to the eternal quest for truth?

As we progress deeper into the realm of the Emerald Tablets, the line between artifact and myth blurs further. Discovering their existence was just the beginning; the true quest lies in deciphering their wisdom. With each insight and artifact uncovered, the legacy of Thoth beckons forward, insisting that the search for understanding never truly ends. In this discovery, we find the promise of transformation — a passage through which the wisdom of ancient times might breathe new life into our modern world.

Archaeological Insights into the Tablets

The quest to uncover the Emerald Tablets wasn't just about finding ancient artifacts; it was a journey through layers of time deeply connected to Thoth's enduring legacy. The archaeological milieu offers a fascinating glimpse into how these mystical tablets were unearthed and studied, revealing the profound connections between legend and reality. These excavations transformed myths into tangible history, providing scholars with a basis to explore the enigmatic teachings attributed to Thoth and their esoteric wisdom.

Some discoveries occurred in unexpected places, often riddled with complexities and challenges. The environments where the tablets were reportedly found often mirrored the mysteries inscribed upon their surfaces. Archaeologists employed meticulous techniques, leaving no stone unturned, to ensure they preserved every ounce of historical integrity embedded within these ancient scripts. The physical journey through excavation sites felt much like the spiritual journey one experiences when delving into the tablets' teachings—a path laden with layers of understanding waiting to be unraveled.

As more fragments and inscriptions surfaced, researchers realized the geological context of these finds could offer vital clues about the civilizations surrounding them. These insights painted vivid pictures of ancient cultures, where Thoth's wisdom permeated every facet of life. This context wasn't just historical; it was cultural, philosophical, and deeply human. The balance of rigorous scientific methods with a reverence for ancient wisdom allowed archaeologists to not only validate the tablets' origins but also bridge the gap between the mystical and the empirical.

Thus, the discovery of the Emerald Tablets became a pivotal moment, transforming mere curiosity into a deeper quest for knowledge. It invited seekers of wisdom to explore beyond the literal content, urging them to engage with the tablets' teachings as a living

tradition that continues to enlighten and inspire generations. This
archaeological journey, much like Thoth's teachings, is a testament to
the timeless and boundless pursuit of understanding and
enlightenment.

Significant Excavations and Discoveries
As the journey to uncover the mysteries of the Emerald Tablets unfolds, it is the echoes of history that guide modern explorers to these ancient relics. Over several centuries, the pursuit to unearth these enigmatic tablets has been driven not only by archaeologists but also by seekers of ancient wisdom. These quests are often marked by fortuitous discoveries, tantalizing finds that shed light on Thoth's timeless teachings.

One such significant excavation occurred in the early 20th century in the barren sands of Eastern Desert sands near Luxor, Egypt. Archaeologists stumbled upon a burial chamber that seemed ordinary at first. But hidden within its stone walls, they found fragments of what appeared to be ancient script. The language resembled early Coptic at first glance, but as scholars soon realized, these fragments had deeper connections. These symbols were a puzzle, blending elements from Egyptian hieroglyphs and proto-Sinaitic script. The excitement surrounding this discovery was palpable, creating a buzz worldwide. Researchers likened this find to a historical treasure, offering hints into the connections between Egyptian lore and the mystical teachings attributed to Thoth.

This remarkable discovery set off a flurry of expeditions tailored to unveil further such relics. Academic circles began buzzing about the possibility of more hidden chambers in ancient sites long thought to be exhausted of secrets. Explorers, armed with newfound zeal, began re-examining caves, tombs, and temples—spots where Thoth's influence might linger. In one such endeavor, deeper into the Mediterranean basin, a stunning find of gold leaf tablets emerged. These intricate artifacts bore inscriptions echoing the wisdom attributed to the Emerald Tablets, further cementing the threads tying these relics to the mystical phenomena described in ancient texts.

While numerous discoveries acted as pieces of this intricate puzzle, none stirred imagination more than the revelation of a silken scroll found carefully tucked within a clay jar, dating back to antiquity beyond clear record. This scroll, when unfurled, illustrated scenes of a scribe capturing what seemed to be Thoth's teachings. The imagery carved onto the vellum spoke in riddles yet glowed with sagacity—the hallmark of the Emerald Tablets' narrative. Scholars, mystics, and historians delved into its depths, hoping to extract layers of meaning and uncover ties to broader spiritual doctrines that have influenced cultures through the ages.

The narrative woven by these discoveries is rich and evolving. Each artifact, whether a fragmented tablet or a perfectly preserved scroll, adds texture to our understanding of these mystical writings. They don't merely stand as relics of a distant past but connect us to the ethical and philosophical musings that have traversed epochs. These finds are more than historical footnotes; they are bridges across time, inviting us to explore not just their physical form but the subsequent ideas they've ignited across civilizations. The excavations, far from being an end, are a doorway into the dimensional expanse of human thought, forever changed by the whispering voices of a bygone era.

The Journey from Legend to Artifact

The Emerald Tablets have long captured the imagination of seekers and scholars alike, their journey from legend to artifact shrouded in mystery and intrigue. These enigmatic relics, said to house the universal truths articulated by the wise Thoth, have traveled through time in whispered stories and shadowy myths—becoming more than mere stone or metal, but carriers of profound insight. How they transitioned from being mere legend to tangible artifacts is a fascinating odyssey that reflects both the resilience of truth and the transformative power of the human spirit.

The earliest whispers of the Tablets arise from the mists of antiquity, where they were nothing more than fabled accounts carried across generations. Embedded in the lore of ancient Egypt and recounting the wisdom of Thoth, the god of knowledge and writing, they were said to contain insights so profound that they had to be protected through myth. As the centuries passed, these legends diffused across cultures, morphing in form and substance, yet retaining a core that resonated deeply with each society's seekers of truth.

Legend began its metamorphosis into artifact through meticulous revelations and the relentless curiosity of archaeologists and historians who labored under scorching suns and within the damp confines of forgotten chambers. The physical search for the Tablets wasn't just an act of excavation; it was a journey into the human psyche, where myth holds sway over reason. Every trowel stroke and dirt sift brought these legends one step closer to being grounded in the tactile reality of human history.

Significant discoveries began to surface, often tucked within the broader explorations of Egyptian ruins. These findings suggested that these Tablets weren't just figments of collective imagination. Among ancient scripts and carvings, depictions and references to the Emerald Tablets emerged, giving credence to the idea that such pieces might truly exist beyond myth. Each deciphered symbol told a story of a time when knowledge was guarded zealously, when it was believed that understanding the universe's workings could elevate humanity to a new realm of enlightenment.

As tales were compared and analyzed alongside extant artifacts, a narrative began to emerge that suggested the Tablets might have been passed between diverse cultures—each contributing their interpretation while preserving an essential core. Thus, the legend evolved, branching into various traditions, yet maintaining the allure of near-mythical wisdom. And so, the scholarly journey from speculation to discovery unfolded, fraught with equal measures of frustration and revelation.

This narrative isn't just an archaeological one; it's deeply philosophical. The transition from legend to artifact challenges us to reconsider how we perceive truths hidden beneath layers of time and translation. The existential question becomes poignant: Were the Tablets merely a metaphor for universal truths or tangible objects that recorded such insights? This intersection of belief and evidence invites us to engage with both the tangible and the intangible aspects of ancient wisdom.

The gradual unveiling of these artifacts also serves as a reminder of the fragility of wisdom amid the sands of time. What persists—be it stone, metal, or myth—is the enduring quest for understanding. As layers of history are peeled back, revelations often lead to more questions than answers, underscoring the Tablets' power to continually inspire and confound. The essence of the Tablets lies in their ability to bridge the chasm between the known and the unknown, urging us to embrace the mysteries that lie beyond our grasp.

Reflecting on this journey from legend to artifact, we find ourselves at a crossroads of past and present. This narrative isn't just about uncovering ancient relics; it's about the perpetual human quest to connect with timeless truths. The transformation from myth to reality invites us to honor all those who dared to seek, who challenged the known boundaries of their time to uncover an ancient wisdom that continues to captivate and illuminate.

Chapter 3: Decoding the Emerald Tablets

To delve into the cryptic writings of the Emerald Tablets is to embark on a journey where ancient wisdom meets modern curiosity. Unlike other texts that may reveal their secrets with a straightforward gaze, the Tablets demand a deeper engagement—a decoding, if you will, of their enigmatic verses. Encoded within these compact lines is a treasury of themes and symbols, each a key to a larger cosmic understanding.

The Tablets are a miraculous tapestry woven with the threads of alchemical symbology, esoteric wisdom, and mythic sequences. One can't help but be struck by their ability to capture universal truths with such brevity and elegance. They speak of a cosmic unity, a grand oneness that transcends the dualistic nature of earthly existence. In this, they echo the wisdom of Thoth himself. Through the ciphered verses, we glimpse notions of balance and transformation that are essential to the human experience.

The themes in the Tablets repeatedly emphasize transformation. This is not just an individual metamorphosis but a cosmic dance between energies. Here, the symbolism of gold, lead, and the philosopher's stone emerges—a metaphor for the alchemical journey. The imagery of the hero's journey, of death and rebirth, mirrors this transformation. The adept becomes the philosopher, and the lead of the base self is transmuted into the gold of enlightenment. Such metaphors speak to both the literal alchemists and the spiritual seekers among us.

As seekers, we become the alchemists of our own lives, guided by the symbology within these texts. Words such as "immortality" and "light" resound through the Tablets, challenging us to redefine our understanding of these concepts. But these are not commandments or doctrines; rather, they are mirrors inviting reflection. The depth within simplicity here is profound, enticing one to ponder the very fabric of reality.

The linguistic texture of the original language itself adds another layer to the complexity of the Emerald Tablets. Written in archaic language, the words resonate with a rhythm that evokes a sense of the divine. They were crafted in a time quite removed from our own, yet their messages remain timeless. Much of the mystique comes from the translation process itself, where the art of capturing the essence of the original while engaging with the ever-evolving nature of language provides its own form of alchemy.

Scholars engage in endless debates over the true meanings of specific words and phrases, each translation offering a slightly different nuance or perspective. Is the light within these sentences truly literal, or is it the illumination of knowledge that they imply? These questions lead to further unraveling of the Tablets, each interpretation bearing new fruit for the inquisitive mind.

Observing the Tablets through a modern linguistic lens reveals as much about us as about the ancient scribes. Today's interpretations bring to light our own cultural biases and intellectual leanings. By striving to comprehend the original language, we are also decoding ourselves in a way, merging past with present. There's a bridge here, linking yesterday's wisdom with today's thirst for understanding, urging us to think beyond the words and to consider the intangible essence they might be conveying.

As we continue our exploration of these arcane texts, let us remain open to the realization that no single interpretation holds monopoly over truth. The Emerald Tablets reward those willing to accept ambiguity and complexity. In our world of instant answers, they stand as a testament to the journey of discovery rather than the destination. We are left not with a set of instructions, but with a guide—one that prompts us to peel back layers of symbolism and language in search of our own enlightenment.

Thus, "Decoding the Emerald Tablets" becomes not just an academic exercise, but a personal voyage. It calls for an open heart as much as an eager mind. Each verse, each chosen word, is a piece of the greater mystery, urging us to decode not just the secrets of the past, but also those within ourselves. This is where the true legacy of the Emerald Tablets resides: in their perpetual invitation to seek, to learn, and ultimately, to transform.

Key Themes in the Tablets' Writings

The Emerald Tablets, shrouded in mystery and glowing with timeless wisdom, reveal a tapestry of themes that weave together the esoteric and the universal. Central to their writings is the concept of unity, where the microcosm reflects the macrocosm, urging seekers to find harmony within themselves and the cosmos. Embedded deep in the lines is the call for personal transformation, guided by the principles of alchemy not just in the physical sense, but at a spiritual level, inviting readers to transcend ordinary limitations. These texts emphasize the eternal journey of the soul, encouraging a continual cycle of learning and growth, challenging initiates to unlock the hidden potential within. Through their cryptic language, the Tablets whisper the secrets of cosmic laws, encouraging a dance with the mysteries of life, urging us to embrace the balance between light and darkness. Such are the lessons that echo down the ages, as we decode their encoded wisdom, forever relevant to the quest for meaning in our modern lives.

Symbolism and Metaphors in the Text, like the artful strokes of an ancient painter, reveal the rich tapestry interwoven throughout the mysterious writings of the Emerald Tablets. In studying these cryptic texts, we begin to uncover layers of meaning beneath the surface. These layers offer deeper insights into the wisdom that has captivated seekers of esoteric knowledge for centuries.

The Emerald Tablets are famously attributed to Thoth, an enigmatic figure often depicted with the head of an ibis and revered as the god of writing and wisdom in ancient Egyptian culture. This imagery itself is a potent symbol, reflecting Thoth's dual role as both scribe and sage. The ibis symbolizes knowledge through observation, with its long, probing beak that echoes the process of seeking deeper understanding. The intersection of animal and divine in Thoth serves as a metaphor for the merging of earthly and spiritual wisdom, setting the stage for the rich symbolism embedded within the text of the Tablets.

In the Tablets, there exists a constant interplay between light and darkness, a theme prevalent across many ancient traditions. Light is often depicted as a symbol of knowledge, enlightenment, and the divine, while darkness may represent ignorance, the unknown, or the material world that obscures higher truths. This duality isn't just illustrative; it guides the reader through a journey of awakening, encouraging introspection and the quest to bring light into one's own understanding. The metaphor of light penetrating the darkness serves as an allegory for the process of spiritual illumination, a central motif within the teachings of the Emerald Tablets.

One of the symbolic frameworks in the Tablets is the concept of the "as above, so below" principle, which posits that the microcosm reflects the macrocosm. This Hermetic axiom is crucial in understanding the interconnectedness of all things. It suggests that the operations of the heavens find echoes in the terrestrial world, inviting us to see the divine order mirrored in the mundane. Through this lens, the Tablets encourage a holistic view of the universe, urging the seeker to discern patterns of truth and harmony that are constant across all levels of existence.

Metaphors within the Emerald Tablets also draw extensively on alchemical themes of transformation. Just as base metals were believed to be transmuted into gold, the spiritual seeker is called to embark on an inner alchemy, refining the soul through wisdom and experience. This metaphor of transformation is more than just a literal quest for immortality; it suggests a profound journey of personal evolution, where the self is continuously reshaped and elevated toward a higher state of being.

Within this context, the myth of the "Philosopher's Stone" emerges as a powerful symbol. It represents the ultimate goal of the alchemical process, not just in physical terms but spiritually—a metaphor for the attainment of enlightenment and eternal life. The elusive Stone embodies the eternal quest for perfection, urging seekers to cultivate both patience and perseverance in their pursuit of truth.

The symbolism of the serpent entwines through the text as well, rooted in ancient iconography with the serpent often portrayed as a guardian of sacred knowledge and a symbol of wisdom. In the Tablets, the serpent may be seen as an emblem of the cyclical nature of life and the perpetual renewal of wisdom and understanding. The shedding of its skin reflects the idea of continuous growth and transformation, mirroring the spiritual rebirth the Tablets advocate.

Nature itself stands out as a central metaphor. The elements are not merely constituents of the physical world but are seen as embodiments of deeper, universal principles. Earth, air, fire, and water each possess both literal and allegorical significance, representing facets of the human experience and spiritual progression. Fire, for instance, is a recurrent symbol of purification and energy, illustrating the quintessential force that drives enlightenment and change.

Another compelling metaphor is the "Great Work," a term borrowed from alchemy that encapsulates the spiritual journey described within the Tablets. This metaphor extends beyond the practice of alchemy to embrace the broader quest for self-realization and divine union. The Great Work is a lifelong pursuit, one that requires dedication, insight, and an alignment of one's actions with universal truth—a concept that continues to resonate with modern spiritual seekers.

The Tablets frequently employ natural imagery to convey their messages, each natural symbol offering a glimpse into the workings of the cosmos. For instance, the balance and harmony found in ecosystems are often reflective of the balance sought within oneself. In recognizing these parallels, readers are encouraged to harmonize their inner world with the outer, fostering a sense of unity with the universe.

Symbolism in the Tablets often invokes the concept of the eternal and cyclical nature of life. Concepts of life, death, and rebirth are illustrated through the metaphor of the phoenix, a mythical bird that rises anew from its ashes. This vivid image embodies the Tablets' teachings on the regeneration of spirit and continuous renewal, resonating with the cyclical rhythms observed in nature—the cycles of the moon, the changing of seasons, and the lifecycle of living beings.

Moreover, the contentment and fulfillment that come from achieving wisdom are often metaphorically represented as a form of nourishment—a spiritual feast that sustains the seeker throughout their journey. This metaphor invites reflection on the sustenance provided by knowledge and suggests that true fulfillment is found not in material wealth but in spiritual abundance.

Throughout the Emerald Tablets, the interplay of symbols and metaphors provides not only depth but also accessibility to its profound teachings. These literary devices serve as keys, unlocking the mysteries within, allowing us to appreciate the timeless wisdom the Tablets offer. In embracing their allegorical language, we partake in a form of meditation, one that guides us toward a holistic transformation of body, mind, and spirit, echoing the essence of the ancient truths they seek to convey.

Linguistic Analysis of the Original Language

The Emerald Tablets, steeped in mystery and enigma, invite us into a linguistic labyrinth where each word dances with ancient legacy and divine inspiration. The language of these tablets is not merely a vehicle for conveying messages but a living vessel that holds the mysteries of time. It is in this language that one begins to decode the true essence of Thoth's wisdom, unlocking the secrets embedded within each carved inscription.

Understanding the tablets' original language requires us to journey back through time, reaching beyond the sands of Egypt and into the cradle of civilization where language was first molded. The text of the Emerald Tablets is often considered to have origins in the ancient tongues of both Egyptian and perhaps even Sumerian languages, echoing a time when oral history began transitioning into written form. It's through this lens that we start piecing together the linguistic puzzle, recognizing its intricacies and the profound depth it carries. Here, the power of language is revealed not just in what is said, but how even the subtlest nuance carries timeless wisdom.

The choice of language in the Emerald Tablets isn't merely a matter of formality. It is deeply symbolic, perhaps even mimicking the alchemical transformation that the tablets themselves speak of. Ancient languages were often imbued with layers of meaning; a single word or phrase could carry a spectrum of interpretations. Thoth, the mythical scribe of the gods, is said to have deliberately crafted his messages to encapsulate profound spiritual truths, wrapped in such linguistic richness that unfolds like a lotus under the discerning mind's gaze.

Yet, the understanding of this sacred text demands more than a simple translation—it requires interpretation and introspection. Not only does each word need to be thoroughly examined within its historical context, but it must also be appreciated for its symbolic value. This dual approach uncovers the experiential knowledge—the paths through which one connects with the divine. The linguistic framework the tablets present is a gateway to a broader philosophy of existence, inviting each seeker to explore beyond the superficial into the very essence of Thoth's teachings.

Furthermore, the tablets' language displays a unique syntactical structure that reveals much about ancient communication practices. The rhythm and meter found in these inscriptions often resemble poetic verse, suggesting that they were meant to be recited, resonating in the souls of those who heard them. This rhythmic quality serves not only as a mnemonic device but also as an invitation to engage with the words on a meditative level, allowing the seeker to truly absorb and reflect on their meaning.

The linguistic elements of the tablets bear resemblance to ancient Egyptian hieroglyphics, where symbols and sounds merge to form an intricate script that speaks to more than the literal world—it reaches into the metaphysical. The tablets utilize metaphors and allegory, employing a style that often hides more than it reveals on the first reading. This intentional obfuscation encourages the reader to ponder, meditate, and return to the text repeatedly, each time uncovering new layers of insight.

In the context of the modern era, engaging with the language of the Emerald Tablets becomes an exercise in both scholarship and spiritual exploration. While translations into contemporary languages have offered accessibility, many scholars argue that nothing can replace the profound experience of attempting to understand the tablets in their original form. It's akin to hearing a symphony in full orchestration rather than through a recording, providing an experience that transcends mere intellectual understanding to touch the soul.

The challenge of preserving the integrity of the original language is monumental, as each phrase in the tablets carries a multiplicative potential for both meaning and misinterpretation. It's a linguistic tapestry woven with precision, demanding that to fully comprehend it, one must recognize the beauty in its ambiguity and embrace the uncertainty it represents. The essence of Thoth's teachings may be hidden in plain sight, waiting for the minds and hearts open to the whispers of forgotten languages.

In conclusion, the linguistic analysis of the original language of the Emerald Tablets is a profound and ongoing endeavor. It requires a balance of philological skill, historical insight, and spiritual openness. By exploring the language of these ancient texts, we not only seek to understand the message conveyed by Thoth but also to awaken a deeper connection to the mysteries that transcend time and continue to inspire those who dare to ponder their own place within the universe. The language of the Emerald Tablets, though ancient, remains a powerful beacon, illuminating the path for seekers willing to delve into its ageless wisdom.

Chapter 4: The Teachings of Thoth

As we delve into the teachings of Thoth, we step into a realm where the lines between myth and wisdom blur, giving rise to profound insights. Thoth, known in antiquity as the scribe of the gods and the master of knowledge, offers a mosaic of wisdom that intertwines cosmic principles with the personal journey of enlightenment. His teachings, as immortalized in the Emerald Tablets, present a tapestry of truth—woven from threads of light and shadow, magic and logic, science and spirituality.

In the heart of these tablets lies a core that speaks to the eternality of knowledge—a principle suggesting one's path isn't merely a linear progression but rather a spiral, ever-reaching, ever-deepening. Thoth presents time as a circle, an ouroboros eating its own tail, returning again and again to the roots of wisdom while spiraling outward into new manifestations. This cyclical understanding contrasts with the modern fixation on linear goals, pushing us to consider our lives as part of a greater continuum.

One might ask, how do these ancient principles relate to us today, thousands of years removed from Thoth's epoch? The timelessness of his teachings suggests that wisdom is not bound to any specific era or culture. The Emerald Tablets embody universal truths that transcend temporal bounds, encouraging introspection and transformation on both a personal and collective level.

The essence of Thoth's teachings often gravitates around the harmonization of opposites, imploring us to find the synthesis between dual forces—light and dark, life and death, creation and destruction. Such duality is not meant to exist isolated but as coordinates on the spectrum of experience. By integrating these polarities, we cultivate balance and harmony within ourselves and in our interactions with the world.

In ancient schools of thought, Thoth's influence loomed large, where his wisdom fed the fertile grounds of disciplines like philosophy, mathematics, and metaphysics. Scholars and initiates alike sought enlightenment through his guidelines, discovering the intricate dance between intellect and mystery. Even the Pythagorean and Platonic traditions echo Thoth's teachings in their pursuit of unity in multiplicity and the harmony of the cosmos.

Practical applications of Thoth's teachings are abundant. Consider the emphasis on self-knowledge, as captured in the maxim "Know thyself," an imperative that invites us into the depths of our consciousness. This exploration, guided by Thoth's wisdom, leads to an understanding that unlocks potentials hidden within our very being. By aligning with the macrocosm's rhythms, individuals can enact transformation not only in themselves but also in society at large.

Furthermore, the teachings advocate the power of words and symbols. Words act as conduits, tools that can construct or dismantle. Thoth, the god of language and writing, manifested this idea by crafting language as an instrument to shape reality, a nod to the creative power housed within every syllable uttered. Indeed, the ability to articulate is a divine gift, one that encourages us to create with intention and awareness.

To draw from Thoth's lessons requires a blend of reflection, practice, and intuition. It invites us to step beyond the confines of everyday perception and engage with the mysteries that lie beneath. As one peels back the layers of mundane routine, they reveal the sacred hidden within, a masterful key to inner revolution and societal evolution.

Thoth's teachings continue to hold sway not only for their ancient allure but also for their capacity to align humanity with a universal rhythm. It's this alignment that fosters a shift from chaos to order, from ignorance to understanding. In a world perpetually tilted towards advancement at any cost, these teachings reignite the call for balance, urging us to recognize the interconnectedness of all things.

As we unravel the wisdom of these teachings, may we carry forward the insights of Thoth, weaving them into the fabric of our lives, nurturing the seeds of enlightenment in our hearts, and extending them into the expansive field of human consciousness. In this way, the ancient voices still whisper to us, guiding each seeker towards a more profound, harmonious existence—an existence embraced by the crystalline clarity found within the Emerald Tablets.

Core Principles of Thoth's Wisdom

Thoth, the legendary scribe of the gods, holds a storied place in ancient mythology and esoteric wisdom. The wisdom he imparts through the Emerald Tablets is a beacon of knowledge for seekers drawn to unravel the mysteries of existence. It's a tapestry woven from threads of divine intellect, cosmic laws, and alchemical principles. To truly grasp these core principles is to engage in a dialogue with the universe itself, to hear whispers of the cosmos echoing within one's own soul.

At the heart of Thoth's teachings lies the idea of unity and interconnectedness. He invites us to look beyond the illusion of separateness, urging recognition of the underlying unity that binds all forms of creation. The principle of "as above, so below" encapsulates this idea, suggesting that the microcosm and macrocosm reflect each other. By understanding the cosmos, one can understand the self, and vice versa. This relationship proposes that personal transformation can lead to a broader understanding of universal truths.

Equally important is the pursuit of inner wisdom. For Thoth, the journey towards wisdom isn't solely an intellectual endeavor; it's a transformative path that integrates mind, body, and spirit. Knowledge is but a stepping stone to wisdom, and wisdom itself is a living, breathing pursuit that demands introspection and humility. His teachings emphasize that to become wise, one must cultivate a deep understanding of the self, casting light on one's own shadows and embracing the eternal quest for growth and enlightenment.

Embracing balance is another central principle in Thoth's wisdom. He champions the harmonious interplay of opposites: light and dark, life and death, order and chaos. This duality is not a paradox to be feared but a dynamic balance to be nurtured. Everything in existence holds its counterpart, and every action has its reaction. Thoth teaches that by embracing these opposites, individuals can find equilibrium within themselves and in the world around them.

Underlying this quest for balance is the transformative power of alchemy, a spiritual and philosophical process that Thoth passionately endorsed. Through alchemical transmutation, one can refine the spirit and achieve a higher state of awareness. Alchemy, beyond the literal transformation of base metals into gold, symbolizes the development of personal consciousness and the unlocking of potential. Thoth shows that the path to self-mastery is through constant refinement and evolution.

Furthermore, Thoth underscores the significance of intentional creation. He posits that thoughts are powerful—each one an inception point for reality. By mastering one's thoughts and aligning them with purpose and vision, individuals can mold their destinies. This creative approach suggests that reality itself can be shaped and transformed by enlightened intent, emphasizing mindfulness in thought and action.

The principle of impermanence also weaves through Thoth's teachings. He reminds us that change is the only constant, a relentless tide that shapes and reshapes life. In acknowledging impermanence, one cultivates adaptability and resilience. Life's transient nature should inspire not despair but a conscious appreciation of momentary experiences and the wisdom they bring.

In acknowledging these core principles, Thoth's teachings push us toward personal responsibility. He insists on accountability in thoughts, words, and actions, highlighting the role of free will in shaping one's destiny. Each choice reverberates through the fabric of existence, influencing the self and the universe in a cosmic dance of cause and effect. By taking responsibility for our lives, we become architects of our own realities.

In exploring the core principles of Thoth's wisdom, we encounter a profound call to awaken to our fullest selves. Let those teachings inspire a journey toward knowledge and transformation, challenging us to seek the divine within and in the cosmos. His wisdom is timeless, resonating with the ancient past and beckoning us toward a future of boundless potential. Through embracing these core principles, one doesn't just study the Emerald Tablets—they live them, becoming the living embodiment of Thoth's eternal message.

Influence on Ancient Schools of Thought resonates as a continuation of Thoth's wisdom, deeply interwoven with ancient philosophies that emerged across diverse civilizations. This aspect of his teaching reached Latin and Greek intellects, transecting boundaries both geographical and ideological. Thoth, as the alleged scribe of the gods, bore influence that transcended his Egyptian roots, whispering knowledge into the ears of those who shaped the philosophical foundations of the Western world.

In the corridors of ancient Greece, where thoughts were molded into structured arguments and theories, Thoth's principles reverberated subtly yet profoundly. It's said that the Academy of Athens, established by Plato, harbored threads of Thoth's wisdom woven through its philosophical tapestry. Plato's ideas about ideal forms mirror the clarity and perfection found in Thoth's teachings. It's as if the distilled essence of Thoth's thought managed to seep through the intellectual exchange between Greece and Egypt, perhaps during the times when Greek scholars studied in the temples of Egypt.

Further illustrating Thoth's reach, Pythagoras, the renowned mathematician, and philosopher, allegedly studied in Egypt. The influence of Thoth on Pythagorean thought is evidenced in their mutual appreciation for the harmony and order of the cosmos. Thoth's wisdom, articulated in the mysterious language of symbols and metaphors, finds a parallel in Pythagorean numerology which sees numbers as the fundamental concept of reality. It's a fascinating synergy where sacred geometry and divine wisdom blend, illustrating the cross-pollination of cultural and philosophical ideas.

Not to be overlooked is the influence Thoth had on Hermeticism, a religious and philosophical tradition that developed during the time of the Roman Empire. Hermeticism itself is deeply rooted in the teachings attributed to Hermes Trismegistus, an amalgamation of the Greek god Hermes and Thoth. Here, Thoth's core principles transformed into crucial tenets of Hermetic philosophy, such as the idea of "As above, so below." This reflects the interconnectedness of the universe, echoing Thoth's vision of a coherent, unified existence.

In regions beyond the Mediterranean, the influence spreads further. The early Islamic scholars in places like the House of Wisdom in Baghdad absorbed the Greco-Egyptian wisdom that Germinated in their hands, leading to profound scientific and philosophical advancements during the Islamic Golden Age. Texts rich in Thoth's lore, including pieces like the 'Emerald Tablet,' traversed cultural boundaries, reaching scholars who would translate and build upon these foundational ideas. Their endeavors preserved and expanded the reach of Thoth's teachings, cementing his influence on the evolving intellectual landscapes.

One finds echoes of Thoth's teachings in Eastern philosophies too, where similarities in cosmology and metaphysical principles occur. Although these connections are more thematic and conceptual rather than direct lines of influence, the reflective nature of wisdom throughout human history often reveals similar truths discovered independently. Thoth's core principles of wisdom and the pursuit of knowledge resonate universally, as seen in the enlightening quests across varied civilizations.

In summation, Thoth's wisdom laid a rich groundwork that inspired ancient schools of thought across civilizations. His teachings embodied a form of esoteric bridge, connecting disparate cultures through shared ideas and insights about the universe and human existence. It was in the creative interplay of exchanging knowledge that Thoth's influence blossomed, inspiring thinkers to explore realms of understanding beyond conventional boundaries. In every philosophical discipline that sought to comprehend the mysteries of life, traces of Thoth's enduring legacy can be perceived, silently guiding the seeker toward wisdom. His teachings served as a catalyst, forever igniting the intellectual fires that continue to burn bright in our perpetual quest for knowledge and enlightenment.

Practical Applications of Thoth's Teachings

In the realm of ancient wisdom, the teachings of Thoth stand out like a beacon for those seeking knowledge and insight. Buried within the cryptic yet profound verses of the Emerald Tablets, Thoth's wisdom offers guidance applicable even in contemporary times, transcending the limitations of its ancient context. These teachings provide a framework for understanding life's complexities and a toolkit for personal transformation, inviting individuals to explore their potential and gain deeper insights into the universe's mysteries.

At the heart of Thoth's teachings is the concept of balance and harmony, drawn from the belief that true understanding lies not in extremes but in the equilibrium between them. This principle can be immediately applied to the chaos and dichotomies present in modern life. In today's world, where stress and imbalance are commonplace, finding harmony within and with the external world becomes a pursuit of utmost importance. Thoth's teachings encourage individuals to cultivate a balanced and harmonious mindset, which can lead to improved mental health, reduced stress, and a more fulfilled life.

Furthermore, the thematic emphasis on transformation and renewal in Thoth's teachings provides a pathway for personal development. At a practical level, this translates to the recognition of one's own capacity for change and growth, akin to the process of alchemical transformation. By embracing the changes within and around us, we learn to adapt and evolve rather than resist, echoing Thoth's profound insight into the fluid nature of existence. This alchemical approach to self-improvement allows individuals to turn perceived failures into opportunities for growth, mirroring the transformational journey from base to noble elements outlined in the Tablets.

Communication and interconnectedness are also recurrent motifs in Thoth's teachings, emphasizing the importance of relationships, not only between humans but also with the environment and cosmos. In practical terms, this might mean honing communication skills, fostering empathetic connections, and nurturing a deeper relationship with nature. By understanding the interconnected nature of all things, individuals are encouraged to act with greater awareness and responsibility towards others and the world at large, a practice that holds considerable relevance in tackling global challenges like climate change and social inequality.

Another practical application is found in the pursuit of knowledge, which Thoth champions as a sacred journey. This reverence for continual learning can inspire a lifelong commitment to education and personal enlightenment. Whether through formal education or self-directed exploration, embracing Thoth's call to seek wisdom can lead to enriched lives and a greater capacity to contribute positively to society. This dedication to acquiring knowledge not only aids personal growth but also fuels innovation and progress within various fields.

The principle of self-knowledge, emphasized strongly in Thoth's doctrines, carries practical implications for modern self-discovery and introspection. In an age where identity and authenticity can often be overshadowed by societal expectations and digital personas, Thoth's teachings beckon us to turn inwards to uncover our true selves. Such self-reflection cultivates authenticity, purpose, and alignment with one's values, leading to a more genuine and gratifying existence. This mindful awareness of one's inner life stands as a testament to the timeless relevance of Thoth's insights.

In addition, Thoth's emphasis on the power of words and thoughts is a guiding principle for those navigating the complexities of speech and intention. In a world inundated with information and communication, being conscious of our language's impact carries immense significance. By learning to harness the profound power of words, individuals can improve not only personal interactions but also influence their own mindset and worldview. This awareness can lead to more meaningful dialogues and the creation of a more supportive and positive environment, both internally and externally.

Underlying all of Thoth's teachings is the inherent unity of all things, suggesting that no aspect of life exists in isolation. This perspective fosters a holistic approach to tackling personal and collective challenges, encouraging individuals to appreciate the broader context in which they operate. In practice, this could mean considering the ripple effects of one's actions, fostering interconnected solutions, and striving for collective well-being rather than isolated achievements.

The profound attention given to the cyclical nature of existence within Thoth's teachings sparks contemplation on the patterns that govern life's events. Recognizing these cycles amplifies our understanding of persistence and resilience, essential qualities in navigating life's ups and downs. By applying this cyclical understanding, individuals can better anticipate and respond to life's challenges, learning to ride the waves of change with grace and fortitude.

As we draw teachings from Thoth into the tapestry of contemporary life, it becomes evident that such ancient wisdom provides more than esoteric insight. It offers practical guidance that is both invaluable and applicable today. By embodying these principles, from cultivating balance and transformation to honing communication and self-awareness, the teachings of Thoth can illuminate the path toward a more harmonious and enlightened existence. This pursuit of ancient knowledge thus becomes a deliberate journey towards a future that honors the wisdom of the past while embracing the potential of the present.

Chapter 5: The Alchemical Connection

The allure of alchemy has long entwined itself with the secrets of the Emerald Tablets. As we delve into this enigmatic chapter, we explore the tantalizing possibility that these ancient texts may indeed hold keys to the mysteries of transformation and transmutation. Long before alchemy became a pursuit of the medieval ages, it found its roots in the teachings and symbols of the tablets, casting a shadow that influenced both thought and practice in profound ways.

Alchemy, often dismissed as mere attempts to transmute base metals into gold, holds a deeper spiritual significance. It offers insights into processes of personal transformation, mirroring the soul's journey toward enlightenment. The Emerald Tablets, with their cryptic phrases, compel us to read between the lines, beckoning us to connect the physical with the metaphysical, the seen with the unseen. This connection hints at a universe where change is both inevitable and essential, where the ordinary becomes extraordinary through understanding and intention. Such ideas resonated with practitioners who sought not only material wealth but spiritual emancipation.

Key figures in alchemical history have often drawn inspiration from the Tablets, viewing them as a cornerstone of arcane wisdom. Paracelsus, a towering figure in Renaissance alchemy, revered the Tablets as a guide for his own philosophies, which blended science, magic, and mysticism. The enduring influence of Thoth can be seen in the work of these practitioners, who often perceived their efforts as part of an ancient lineage—a dialogue between past wisdom and present intellect.

The craft of alchemy, with its crucibles and elixirs, symbolizes the journey from ignorance to enlightenment. This transformation reflects the esoteric truths embedded in the Emerald Tablets, urging us toward the pursuit of higher knowledge. In understanding this alchemical connection, we uncover insights that transcend time, inviting a deeper exploration of our potential as seekers of wisdom.

Alchemy's Influence on the Tablets

At the heart of the profound mystery surrounding the Emerald Tablets lies the indelible mark of alchemy. This ancient practice, with its origins steeped in both mysticism and proto-science, finds its echoes within the cryptic inscriptions attributed to Thoth. Alchemy, much like the metaphors woven into the Tablets, is a language of transformation. It embodies the quest for transmutation—not merely of base metals into gold, but of the soul's elevation from the mundane to the divine. The Emerald Tablets speak to this dual nature, revealing wisdom that transcends the material and touches the spiritual essence.

Alchemy's influence over the Tablets is palpable in their enigmatic portrayal of the philosopher's stone, the legendary alchemical substance said to grant immortality. While the stone eludes definitive identification, its symbolic significance cannot be overstated. It represents the culmination of the alchemical process—the ultimate goal of personal enlightenment and unity with the divine. Through allegory and symbolism, the Tablets guide the seeker on a mystical journey mirroring alchemy's own transformational path.

Throughout history, many alchemists have found inspiration in the Tablets' teachings, using them as a lens through which to view their own practices. These texts provided a blueprint, a mystical overlay under which the physical acts of distillation and transformation took on metaphorical weight, shaping the philosophical underpinnings of alchemy. The convergence of Thoth's ancient wisdom with alchemical thought forged a unique tapestry, one that continues to intrigue seekers of esoteric truths. By unraveling these layers, the true essence of alchemy's influence on the Tablets emerges—a timeless pursuit of wisdom, revealing the interconnectedness of all things.

Transformation and Transmutation Concepts within the realm of alchemy have long captivated the minds of those who venture into the depths of ancient wisdom. Rooted in the mysterious teachings of the Emerald Tablets, these concepts are more than mere chemical changes; they represent profound shifts in consciousness and spirit. Alchemy's influence on these enigmatic writings extends beyond the realm of turning base metals into gold, diving instead into the transformative journey of the self. It's a journey that calls seekers to explore the esoteric dimensions of their being and the universe.

At the heart of alchemical teachings lies the principle that transformation is an intrinsic part of both nature and the human experience. The Emerald Tablets amplify this principle by presenting the notion that within everyone resides the potential for profound change. In the transmutation concepts found within, one finds a blueprint for spiritual growth and enlightenment. By aligning with the natural laws as expressed through alchemical symbolism, seekers can transcend ordinary existence and attain a state of higher consciousness.

The transformative journeys depicted in the Tablets do not merely apply to the physical realm. These narratives offer lessons in reshaping one's essence and one's place in the cosmos. Transmutation, in this context, refers not just to a change in form or substance, but to the elevation of the soul. The complex allegories and symbols invite interpreters to delve deep beneath the surface, challenging them to redefine their understanding of life, existence, and purpose.

Some might argue that the concepts of transformation and transmutation in alchemy are symbolic representations of life's inherent dualities—opposing forces that must be reconciled for true understanding and growth. These dualities can manifest as good and evil, light and dark, or spirit and matter. The alchemical process encourages us to balance these forces, creating harmony from discord and wisdom from confusion.

For the dedicated seeker, transformation is an ongoing process, not a destination. The Emerald Tablets speak to the perpetual cycle of growth, destruction, and renewal—a concept encapsulated in the ancient maxim: "As above, so below; as within, so without." This Hermetic principle, derived from the Tablets, emphasizes unity and correspondence between the macrocosm and microcosm, underscoring the notion that personal transformation impacts the larger cosmic order.

In the pursuit of spiritual enlightenment, the alchemist embarks on both an inner and outer journey. Armed with the teachings of the Emerald Tablets, these travelers on the path of wisdom follow a path akin to the allegorical journey of lead becoming gold. Yet, it's not in the material wealth they seek their satisfaction, but in the rarified understanding of universal truth that will change their lives.

The story of transformation within the Tablets is also a testament to human potential. It presents an opportunity to reflect on the ways we can transform our understanding of self. By engaging with these ancient texts, individuals can come to a deeper recognition of their own innate abilities to transcend their limitations and achieve greater harmony with the universe.

Transmutation, as highlighted in the Tablets, appeals to the mystical aspect of alchemy, one that operates on symbolism as much as on actual practice. Gold, in its symbolic form, often signifies the spiritual purity sought by the alchemist, rather than material wealth. Such symbolism presents the ripe opportunity for personal reinterpretation and validation of spiritual pursuits within the sacred connection of the alchemical process.

The Emerald Tablets also suggest that transformation is not something that happens in isolation. It occurs through interaction, through relation—be it with the divine, the cosmos, or the self. The inherent transmutation that begins in the inner world inevitably spills over into interactions with the outer world, leading to transformations in society's collective consciousness.

This pervasive influence of alchemical concepts in the Tablets challenges us to not only seek personal transformation but also to contribute to the betterment of the larger world. The alchemist, through their own transformation, becomes a beacon of change, capable of awakening the transformative potential in others.

The writings embedded in the Emerald Tablets serve as a timeless reminder of the ceaseless dance of transformation and transmutation in our lives. By aligning ourselves with these perennial teachings, we hold the keys to unlocking our true potential and discovering the wisdom within. As seekers dive into these ancient waters, they are encouraged to trust the unfolding of their transformation, both seen and unseen.

Historical Alchemy Practitioners Inspired by Thoth

In the swirling mists of time and the transient nature of human understanding, alchemy stands out as both a science and an art. Its enigmatic processes and philosophical underpinnings have fascinated seekers of wisdom for centuries. Among the figures who pursued this ancient craft, the influence of Thoth, the fabled author of the Emerald Tablets, loomed large. His teachings, which spoke of transformation and the unity of all things, offered a rich vein of inspiration for those dedicated to unlocking the mysteries of the material and spiritual worlds.

Thoth, often depicted as a wise scribe with the head of an ibis, was revered in ancient Egyptian culture as the god of wisdom, writing, and science. His legendary works, including the Hermetic Corpus and the Emerald Tablets, provided a spiritual and intellectual foundation for the practice of alchemy. Practitioners who claimed to draw from Thoth's knowledge believed in the possibility of transmuting not only metals but the human spirit itself. This transformative ideal was at the heart of alchemical practice, heavily influencing the prominent alchemists across history.

One of the most renowned of these figures was Hermes Trismegistus, a legendary syncretic combination of the Greek god Hermes and the Egyptian Thoth. His name became synonymous with wisdom and was believed to have authored a vast body of knowledge, including the Corpus Hermeticum. While historians debate the historicity of Hermes Trismegistus, the impact of his attributed works on medieval and Renaissance alchemy was profound. Through these writings, alchemists were introduced to ideas central to Hermeticism, such as the principle of "as above, so below," which spoke to the interconnectedness of all existence. This principle guided alchemists in their quest for the philosopher's stone, a substance said to grant eternal life and the transmutation of base metals into gold.

Paracelsus, a Swiss physician and alchemist of the Renaissance, is another figure who drew upon Hermetic principles. He rejected the Aristotelian and scholastic traditions dominant in European universities at the time, advocating instead for a medical and philosophical system informed by direct observation and experimentation, in line with the teachings understood to be from Thoth. Paracelsus believed that understanding the divine essence within the natural world was key to both healing and transformation. This approach marked a significant shift in alchemical thought, emphasizing the microcosm and macrocosm's unity, a core idea resonant with Thoth's ancient wisdom.

Meanwhile, in the courts of Europe, alchemy thrived as a noble pursuit entwined with mysticism and the quest for knowledge. John Dee, an English mathematician and alchemist in the court of Queen Elizabeth I, exemplified this. Influenced by Hermetic texts attributed to Thoth, Dee pursued alchemy not just as a chemical endeavor but as a spiritual quest. He sought to commune with angels and decipher the divine order of the universe, bridging the gap between the material and spiritual realms, much like Thoth's own teachings suggested. Dee's efforts, though critiqued by his contemporaries, underscored the period's intense fascination with the possibilities of alchemy as a means to transcend human limitations.

The Italian Renaissance also produced figures like Marsilio Ficino, who played a crucial role in reviving Platonic and Hermetic philosophies. Ficino translated the Corpus Hermeticum into Latin, making these texts widely accessible throughout Europe. The translations resonated deeply with scholars and alchemists, encouraging a revival of interest in the spiritual dimensions of alchemy. Ficino's work illustrated the enduring appeal of Thoth-inspired philosophies, which saw the universe as a living entity imbued with divine wisdom.

In the Islamic world, the alchemical tradition prospered with the influence of Thoth palpable in the works of Jabir ibn Hayyan, known as Geber in the West. Considered one of the most influential alchemists of the Islamic Golden Age, Jabir's teachings emphasized the mystical aspects of alchemy, integrating spiritual beliefs with scientific processes. His works, infused with Hermetic ideas, explored the transformation of matter and the purification of the soul, paralleling Thoth's own teachings in the Emerald Tablets.

This profound and enduring impact of Thoth's wisdom across different cultures and time periods highlights the universal appeal of alchemical practice. The blending of mystical and practical pursuits, as embraced by these historical alchemists, mirrored the alchemical axiom of "solve et coagula," to dissolve and to coagulate, the perpetual cycle of breaking down and rebuilding. For Thoth-inspired practitioners, this was not just about physical transformation but an allegory for personal and spiritual evolution, aligning with the deeper truths of existence conveyed through the tablets.

The enduring legacy of Thoth within alchemy serves not only as a testament to the rich tapestry of human curiosity and spiritual ambition but also as an inspiration for modern seekers of wisdom. His teachings, traversing centuries through the works of historical figures, continue to call to those drawn to the mysteries of life, urging them to explore the unseen connections between the material and the mystic. The alchemical practitioners, inspired by Thoth, remind us that the quest for understanding goes beyond the physical realm; it's an inward journey seeking the unity of soul, science, and spirit.

As we delve deeper into the historical tapestry of alchemy, Thoth's influence becomes a guiding light, encouraging both ancient and modern alchemists to transcend the surface and seek the hidden truths of the universe. The Hermetic legacy of transformation and unity, as illustrated by these historical figures, remains a cornerstone in the pursuit of esoteric knowledge, forever intertwined with the enigmatic allure of alchemy and the mystical wisdom of Thoth.

Chapter 6: Hermetic Philosophy and Thoth

In the tapestry of esoteric thought, Hermetic philosophy weaves a narrative that harkens back to times immemorial. Central to this intricate pattern is Thoth, the scribe of the gods, the bearer of wisdom, and the architect of knowledge. As we delve into this chapter, we encounter philosophical principles not just as abstract theories, but as living truths that have journeyed through the echoes of history. From the dimly lit chambers of ancient Egypt to the enlightened halls of the Renaissance, Thoth's teachings have persisted, resonating with those who seek understanding beyond the mundane.

At the core of Hermetic philosophy lies the recognition of unity, the idea that all things are interconnected. This principle, known as "The All," posits that the universe is a single, living organism, reverberating with consciousness. Here, Thoth's influence becomes palpable. His writings suggest a universe bound by connections that transcend the visible, inviting seekers to embrace the unseen. Such beliefs challenge us to perceive beyond the material, encouraging a deeper scrutiny, an introspective exploration.

Consider the Principle of Correspondence, an essential tenet derived from Hermetic thought: "As above, so below; as below, so above." It invites us to understand that the macrocosm and microcosm reflect one another, forming a mirror through which hidden truths are revealed. Thoth, through his legendary tablets, imparts this wisdom with an enigmatic clarity that has inspired countless generations. It invites meditation, a contemplation on the nature of reality itself. When we grasp this idea, the boundaries between worlds blur, revealing the mystic threads that bind all.

The evolution of Hermetic doctrines cannot be discussed without acknowledging the key figures who perpetuated Thoth's wisdom throughout history. Visionaries such as Hermes Trismegistus—the esoteric embodiment of Thoth—appear time and again, echoing these ancient truths. They carried forth the Hermetic message, ensuring that Thoth's insights reached not only priests and scholars but also artists and thinkers who yearned for a glimpse of the divine.

In tracing the paths of those who walked before us, we find that their discoveries become our guiding lights. The Hermetic principles serve as a compass that directs the soul towards enlightenment, challenging us to question the known, explore the unknown, and harmonize the two. These teachings are more than relics of a forgotten time. They are alive, breathing within the sanctum of the present moment, urging us to transcend our limitations and align with the universal mind.

Thus, as we move forward on this journey into Hermetic philosophy and Thoth's timeless wisdom, we embark not only on an exploration of the past but on a revelation of the present. The teachings etched in emerald, guided by Thoth's hand, continue to stir the depths of the human spirit, offering profound insights into the nature of existence. This chapter serves as a doorway, inviting seekers to step through and ponder the vast mysteries that lie beyond, eternally beckoning to those daring enough to seek.

Hermetic Doctrines Derived from the Tablets

Among the whispers of time, the Hermetic doctrines rise as profound echoes of an ancient intellect, casting their shadow from the Emerald Tablets into the very fabric of Hermetic philosophy. These doctrines are not mere remnants of an obscure past; they are living wisdom, intertwined with the essence of Thoth, the Egyptian god associated with wisdom and writing. From these revered texts, unending streams of insight have flowed, nurturing the minds and spirits of those who seek the hidden truths of the universe.

Positioned at the heart of Hermetic teachings is the concept of *All is One*. This central doctrine finds its roots in the Tablets, articulating a vision where every aspect of the universe is interconnected. In this cosmic tapestry, nothing stands alone. Planets, stars, humans, and animals are all threads of the same cloth, each vibration resonating with the others. It is an awakening—an invitation to see beyond dichotomies and embrace the underlying unity that governs all. This perceived unity mirrors the Hermetic Principle of Correspondence, encapsulated in the enigmatic maxim, "As above, so below; as below, so above."

Beyond mere philosophical musings, the Hermetic doctrines address the transformation of the self, an inward alchemy that precedes external alchemy. The notion of 'know thyself' echoes through the ages, urging seekers to journey inward. It speaks of a deep introspective process, intimately intertwined with the mind's ability to reshape reality. Those who walk the Hermetic path understand that this self-awareness is a crucible for spiritual evolution. The Emerald Tablets offer cryptic yet powerful insights into this transformative process, urging individuals to assimilate wisdom personally before attempting to alter external circumstances.

The universality of these doctrines is apparent in their enduring appeal. They resonate with seekers across time and culture, suggesting an innate human longing for deep comprehension and spiritual elevation. Hidden in the veiled language of the Tablets is an invitation to find harmony within oneself and the cosmos. This harmony, when cultivated, shapes internal and external worlds, reflecting the Hermetic belief that transformation begins within. The journey of inner change is likened to the philosopher's stone—a quest to convert the lead of ordinary existence into the gold of spiritual enlightenment.

Central to Hermetic doctrines is the dynamic interplay between the material and the spiritual. The Tablets suggest a dual view of reality where the seen and unseen coalesce, prompting a holistic understanding of existence. Modern science has long championed this duality, bridging gaps between what is known and what is yet to be discovered. Hermetic thinkers embrace this dualism, seeing beyond the physical to grasp the spiritual truths underlying material appearances. Through meditative practices and esoteric rituals, they strive to align themselves with this harmonic balance.

Encoded within the tablets is the art of mental transmutation, a theme deeply embedded in Hermetic principles. This doctrine postulates that the mind is the ultimate alchemical laboratory. Transforming one's thoughts and emotions transforms one's reality—a powerful proposition with roots in the Emerald Tablets. It is in the refining of thought patterns that practitioners find liberation. This potent idea heralds the belief that by mastering the self, one can master the universe.

Communication with the divine, a profound aspect of Hermetic beliefs, finds echoes in the Emerald Tablets. They infer that the divine is not an external entity but an accessible part of the self. To commune with the divine is to reach into the depths of one's essence, uncovering connections to Thoth—messenger of the gods and master scribe. Through prayer, meditation, and reflection, Hermetic practitioners strive to reveal this inner divinity, cultivating insights that guide both practical and spiritual life.

In their cryptic lines, the Tablets offer a moral framework alongside spiritual teachings. They advise on right action, emphasizing the karmic consequence and the pursuit of virtue. The underlying message is clear: moral integrity is inextricably linked to spiritual progress. Ethical conduct aligns one with the forces of harmony and balance, allowing for a clearer reception of cosmic wisdom. This doctrine reinforces the interconnected nature of the Hermetic worldview, asserting that personal morality has universal repercussions.

The doctrines of Hermeticism derived from the Emerald Tablets are expansive, their influence woven through the annals of philosophical and spiritual thought. From ancient wisdom schools to the birth of the Renaissance, their echoes continue to inspire and challenge modern seekers. In our era, the allure of these teachings remains vibrant, suggesting that Thoth's instructions are not mere historical artifacts but living tenets capable of guiding humanity towards a deeper understanding of itself and the universe.

In grasping the doctrines within the Emerald Tablets, we embark on a quest—a sacred pilgrimage through mind and spirit. Each teaching is a beacon, illuminating the path to unity, transformation, and divine understanding. As we tread this path, the wisdom of the ancients slowly unfolds, revealing timeless truths hidden in the emerald-like depths of history. Such is the legacy of the Tablet's Hermetic doctrines, a bridge between the seen and unseen, guiding seekers towards the infinite horizon of knowledge.

The Principle of Correspondence Analysis traces its roots back to the timeless teachings embedded within the Hermetic tradition, bridging the divine and the mundane through the concise yet profound adage: "As above, so below." This belief, birthed from the depths of Thoth's wisdom, serves as a guiding light for seekers of ancient knowledge, offering a lens through which the mysteries of the universe can be discerned. By understanding the Principle of Correspondence, one begins to unravel the interconnected tapestry that weaves together the cosmic and earthly realms.

In every corner of existence, from the minute particles that dance within an atom to the vast galaxies spiraling in the cosmos, the essence of Correspondence reverberates. It reminds us that patterns and truths observed in one plane of reality often mirror those in another. Thoth's teachings suggest that by studying the seen, we can grasp the unseen, allowing us to comprehend the grand design of creation itself. This philosophical cornerstone invites the seeker not only to observe but to discern deeper meanings that lie beneath superficial appearances.

Historically, the Principle of Correspondence has been pivotal in shaping various schools of thought within Hermeticism. Ancient alchemists, inspired by the Emerald Tablets, viewed Correspondence as a key to understanding the transformative processes they sought to master. By recognizing that the inner transformations paralleled outer changes, they endeavored to align their spirit with the divine architecture etched in nature. This acknowledgment facilitated an internal journey of enlightenment and self-discovery, embodying the alchemical maxim of transformation.

Furthermore, the allure of Correspondence captivated mystics and scholars alike, spanning cultures and epochs. It transcended the barriers of language and tradition, underscoring a universal truth that resonated across diverse philosophies. In medieval Europe, the Hermetic texts and the principle they expounded became a beacon of knowledge during the Renaissance, sparking a renewed interest in esoteric studies that intertwined with scientific exploration. This resurgence highlighted the notion that spiritual insights and scientific inquiry are not mutually exclusive but can harmoniously coexist.

The analytical framework offered by the Principle of Correspondence empowers us to explore the dynamic interplay between microcosm and macrocosm. It's not merely a philosophical abstraction; it's a practical tool that can be harnessed in everyday life. By recognizing the patterns that repeat across various domains—be they natural, personal, or societal—we can navigate complexities with greater clarity. This understanding invites a harmonious balance between the internal and external, guiding actions that are in alignment with universal laws.

In practical terms, applying the Principle of Correspondence involves a conscious effort to perceive interconnectedness. It challenges us to seek out synchrony and resonance, to attune our perception to the subtleties of the world around us. Artists, inventors, and visionaries throughout history have wielded this principle intuitively, drawing inspiration from nature to solve human problems. This creative synthesis reflects the very spirit of Hermeticism: the pursuit of wisdom and the elevation of consciousness through awareness of the interlinked worlds.

The prophetic words of the Emerald Tablets echo through the corridors of time, impressing upon the mind of the seeker the significance of Correspondence. Thoth's legacy compels us to look beyond the surface and delve into the depths of our existence to uncover the truths that bind the universe. As we pursue this path illuminated by the teachings of the ancients, we find that the Principle of Correspondence instills a sense of purpose and place in the cosmic order, urging us toward a life of introspection, harmony, and enlightenment.

As modern readers, attuned to the rhythm of contemporary life yet yearning for the wisdom of the ancients, the Principle of Correspondence offers a bridge between worlds. In embracing this principle, we acknowledge the continuous dance of creation and destruction, the rhythm of life that mirrors the celestial movements above. Through this understanding, we glean insights that inspire renewal and transformation, echoing the timeless refrains of Thoth's ageless wisdom.

Key Figures in Hermeticism
Acknowledging Thoth

In the world of Hermetic philosophy, Thoth stands as a beacon of wisdom, his influence extending through millennia. His teachings, encapsulated in the mythical Emerald Tablets, have woven themselves into the fabric of esoteric thought and inspired some of history's most influential figures in Hermeticism. As seekers unravel the mysteries of these profound texts, they encounter illustrious personalities who recognized and revered Thoth's contributions to the mystical arts.

Hermes Trismegistus, an enigmatic figure often identified with Thoth himself, is synonymous with Hermetic thought. This legendary sage is credited with authoring a myriad of works, including the "Corpus Hermeticum," a collection of writings central to Hermetic philosophy. To the followers of Hermetic teachings, Hermes Trismegistus is the human embodiment of Thoth, the divine scribe and keeper of sacred knowledge. His writings emphasize the interconnectedness of all things, a principle that echoes Thoth's teachings on the oneness of the universe.

Plotinus, the celebrated philosopher of the third century, is another luminary inspired by Thoth's wisdom. Although not directly linked with the Hermetic tradition, Plotinus embraced ideas that resonated with the Hermetic principles. His philosophy of Neoplatonism, which seeks the ultimate unity with the divine, mirrors the esoteric quest for enlightenment intrinsic to Thoth's teachings. Through his works, Plotinus influenced early Hermetic thinkers, encouraging them to look beyond the material world to uncover the divine essence within.

In the rich tapestry of Renaissance thought, Marsilio Ficino stands out as a pivotal figure in the revival of Hermeticism. Ficino's translations and commentaries on the "Corpus Hermeticum" revived interest in Thoth's ancient wisdom, breathing new life into these mystical teachings. Ficino perceived Thoth as a critical link between human consciousness and divine understanding, advocating for a synthesis of reason and spirituality—a core tenet shared with Hermetic doctrines.

Another illuminated mind, Giordano Bruno, saw Thoth's teachings as a catalyst for awakening the human spirit. Bruno's vision of an infinite universe, brimming with life and knowledge, finds its echo in the Hermetic principles taught by Thoth. His defiance of conventional doctrines made Bruno a martyr for the cause of knowledge, and his acknowledgment of Thoth as an eternal fountain of inspiration demonstrates the enduring impact of Hermetic wisdom in the face of adversity.

Johannes Kepler, the renowned astronomer, also harbored a fascination for Hermetic thought and Thoth's legacy. While his scientific contributions are widely celebrated, Kepler didn't shy away from drawing upon Hermetic principles in his quest to unlock the cosmos' mysteries. He believed in a harmonious universe governed by divine laws, a view aligning with Thoth's teachings on cosmic order and correspondence. Kepler's work exemplifies the seamless fusion of scientific inquiry with mystical insight, a hallmark of Hermetic tradition.

As the centuries rolled on, the enigmatic figure of Aleister Crowley emerged, channeling Thoth's ancient wisdom into the modern age. Although often controversial, Crowley's exploration of the occult was deeply influenced by Hermetic teachings. The tarot deck he created, "The Book of Thoth," pays homage to the Egyptian god and serves as a tool for spiritual exploration and understanding. Crowley's integration of Thoth's principles underscores the timeless relevance of this wisdom in guiding individuals toward personal transformation.

In contemporary times, Carl Jung, the influential psychiatrist and psychoanalyst, found in Hermeticism a rich source for understanding the human psyche. Jung's exploration of archetypes and the collective unconscious echoes the symbolic language found in Thoth's teachings. He viewed Hermeticism as a repository of spiritual truths that could illuminate the depths of the human soul, acknowledging Thoth as a master of this profound psychological alchemy.

The impact of Thoth on Hermeticism continues to ripple through time, inspiring a diverse array of thinkers, philosophers, and mystics. Each figure, in their unique way, has drawn from Thoth's reservoir of wisdom, interpreting and expanding upon these ancient teachings to navigate their own quests for knowledge. Their acknowledgment of Thoth not only underscores the enduring allure of Hermetic philosophy but also invites modern seekers to delve deeper into the mysteries of the Emerald Tablets and the profound truths they hold.

Chapter 7: The Emerald Tablets in Modern Thought

In an age where the digital and the mystical intertwine like never before, the Emerald Tablets find themselves gleaming afresh in the mind of seekers worldwide. Their teachings, cloaked in antiquity, stretch across time, revealing themselves in new forms, whispering the same ancient truth. Modernity, with all its complexities and challenges, seems to hunger for the depth of wisdom that these ancient writings offer. But why do these tablets, despite their cryptic nature, resonate so profoundly with today's spiritual currents? The answer lies in their timeless relevance and the adaptability of their insight.

Explored through the lens of contemporary spirituality, the Emerald Tablets have found a formidable place in New Age circles. From meditation retreats to online spiritual forums, the concepts of unity and transformation penned by Thoth echo with growing intensity. This movement isn't just a revival; it's an adaptation—a weaving together of ancient wisdom with modern sensibilities. Followers today aren't merely absorbing the teachings; they're actively reinterpreting them to align with sustainable living and holistic practices. It's as if the Tablets' core principles had been lying in wait for present times, their esoteric guidance emerging as a beacon for those navigating the chaos of the 21st century.

Modern interpretations of the Emerald Tablets aren't uniform; they vary as extensively as the individuals who explore them. Yet, within this diversity, one finds a remarkable consensus on the Tablets' emphasis on change and renewal. Many see these concepts mirrored in current psychological and philosophical discussions. Practitioners and theorists might not always explicitly refer to Thoth, but the spirit of his teachings—malleable as ever—inhabits their thoughts. Some liken the Tablets to an ancient psychological model, a precursor to the

Jungian pursuit of individuation or the transformative cycles described by alchemists through the ages.

In some ways, the allure of the Tablets is their poetic dichotomy—both fixed in ancient origins yet fluid in contemporary interpretation. This duality makes them fertile ground for New Age philosophies that prioritize personal evolution and collective consciousness. Thoth's wisdom speaks directly to the idea of interconnectedness, a concept science now explores through the study of fields like quantum physics. To the modern spiritual seeker, such connections suggest that the boundaries between ancient mysticism and cutting-edge science are mere illusions, echoing the Hermetic tenet of 'as above, so below.'

The impact of the Emerald Tablets on New Age movements cannot be overstated. They serve as a foundation for many to re-imagine spirituality as something alive and pertinent, not relics of an ancient past. The Tablets, and through them Thoth, offer a roadmap for interpreting the metaphysical realms in a manner that supports personal and planetary transformation. They're seen as a historical touchstone, inspiring individuals and communities to embrace a global, inclusive perspective, while also urging a deep introspection and understanding of self.

As we unravel the layers of this mystical text—text that can confound and enlighten in equal measure—an invitation is extended: to see the Tablets not as static carved stones, but as living manuscripts that breathe the same life today as they did in an age forgotten by time. Like a tapestry, the Emerald Tablets in modern thought weave historical strands with future-facing innovations. They're not just shaping how we look at spirituality, but also guiding how we understand our ever-evolving role in a universe filled with mystery. Thoth's voice, thus, continues to vibrate through the corridors of time, resonating deeply with those who dare to listen and strive to comprehend.

Relevance in Contemporary Spirituality

In today's rapidly evolving world, many seekers find themselves drawn to the timeless wisdom of ancient texts. The Emerald Tablets, attributed to the mythical figure Thoth, stand out as a beacon for those looking to bridge the ancient and the modern, intertwining the mystical with the pragmatic. As a profound touchstone, they invite today's spiritual explorers to sift through their cryptic teachings and uncover relevant insights that resonate with contemporary life.

The teachings of the Emerald Tablets are not just relics of a bygone era; they're vivid reflections of universal truths that continue to echo through the corridors of time. One might wonder what gives these writings such a lasting impact. It's the way they transcend conventional boundaries, offering insights into personal transformation, spiritual alchemy, and the unity of the cosmos. With such themes, the Tablets speak directly to the core of modern spirituality, which often focuses on personal growth and the search for meaning beyond the material world.

The Tablets' teachings are increasingly valuable amid growing interest in holistic well-being, mindfulness, and the interconnectedness of all things. In an era where individuals actively seek to rise above the confines of day-to-day existence, the Tablets provide a framework for understanding life's cycles, the rhythm of transformation, and the perennial dance between light and darkness. This timeless knowledge offers contemporary seekers a lens through which to view their personal struggles and aspirations as part of a larger, cosmic order.

Many spiritual leaders and new age thinkers have turned to the Emerald Tablets for inspiration, interpreting their esoteric messages to fit modern audiences. By extracting these principles and adapting them to a contemporary context, individuals are empowered to apply these lessons to real-world scenarios, emphasizing integration rather than separation. This inclusive approach allows for personal interpretations that honor the sacred while embracing the present.

Furthermore, as globalization continues its expansive reach, there's a renewed interest in the shared wisdom of humanity's past. The universality found within the Tablets fosters a sense of global unity, transcending cultural and religious divides. This aspect is particularly relevant today, as society becomes more diverse and interconnected. Many find solace in the idea that these ancient teachings promote harmony, suggesting that understanding and mutual respect are pathways to a more enlightened and peaceful world.

The concept of transformation—central to the Emerald Tablets—resonates strongly in today's spirituality, often framed in terms of personal enlightenment or self-actualization. They invite individuals to engage in their own alchemical processes, transforming the base elements of their lives into spiritual gold. This transformative journey, while deeply personal, reflects the collective yearning for higher consciousness, a theme ever-present in the self-help movement and contemporary spiritual practices.

One cannot overlook the profound influence of the Tablets on various new age movements that emphasize holistic, integrative approaches. Practices like meditation, visualization, and energy work often draw from the insights present within these ancient teachings. By grounding contemporary practices in spiritual wisdom, practitioners find deeper meaning and authenticity in their spiritual journey, often reporting enhanced personal fulfillment and peace.

The Tablets also challenge modern thinkers to reconnect with the mystical, urging them to go beyond proof and evidence into the realms of intuition and inner knowing. This is a stark counterpoint to our data-driven culture, encouraging spiritual seekers to trust the insights that arise from deep reflection and meditation. By doing so, they participate in a living tradition, one that bridges the divide between the known and the unknown, the visible and the invisible.

In essence, the Emerald Tablets offer a rich tapestry of wisdom that seamlessly intertwines with the quest for enlightenment in the modern spiritual seeker. They inspire individuals to explore their consciousness, challenging them to cultivate a deeper relationship with the divine mysteries that govern all existence. As we continue to uncover their relevance, the Tablets remind us that the journey inward is as vital today as it was millennia ago.

Modern Interpretations and Adaptations weave a tapestry that connects the cryptic wisdom of the Emerald Tablets with today's quest for spiritual enlightenment. The Tablets, shrouded in mystery and allegory, have been interpreted with fresh eyes to resonate with the ideals of contemporary spirituality. In today's ever-evolving spiritual landscape, seekers gravitate towards ancient wisdom that provides timeless guidance. The Tablet's principle of "As above, so below" has become a beacon for those striving to understand the intricate relationship between the cosmos and personal evolution.

The essence of the Emerald Tablets has found its way into the heart of modern esoteric practices, often through the reinterpretation of its alchemical edicts. Many spiritual practitioners perceive the language of the Tablets as metaphorical, intending to provoke internal transformation akin to the alchemists' quest for turning lead into gold. In more modern terms, this transformation is seen as a shift towards enlightenment or higher consciousness—one of the core aspirations of contemporary spiritual movements.

Moreover, interpretations of the Tablets today often embrace a holistic approach, transcending religious boundaries and fostering a sense of unity and mindfulness. This universal appeal aligns with the

Tablets' enigmatic teachings that have long captivated scholars and mystics alike. The approach is less dogmatic and more experiential, focusing on personal experience and inner realization rather than prescriptive doctrine. Thus, contemporary interpretations often encourage individuals to see the divine aspect within themselves and the universe.

In spiritual circles, the Emerald Tablets are revered not just for their historical mystique but also for their potential to inspire personal growth and transformation. Many modern spiritual teachers use the Tablets to frame dialogues around conscious evolution and the nature of reality. These dialogues often explore the idea that individuals have the ability to shape their own experiences through awareness and intention, reflecting the Hermetic axiom at the core of the Tablets.

Adaptations of the Tablets have also permeated the realm of personal development and self-help. Authors in these fields have distilled the Tablets' complex principles into accessible philosophies for the modern seeker. They highlight the importance of mental clarity, emotional balance, and spiritual fulfillment, aligning these goals with the alchemical process of self-transmutation. As a result, the Tablets' teachings continue to be a source of inspiration for those seeking to actualize their fullest potential.

This modern embrace extends to New Age movements, where the Tablets are often seen as a guiding light for collective consciousness and global awakening. The Tablets have been cited in literature advocating for environmental stewardship, the understanding of cosmic law, and the interconnectedness of all life. This perspective aligns the ancient texts with progressive contemporary thought, suggesting that the Tablets' wisdom can offer solutions to modern existential crises, such as climate change and societal disconnect.

The enigmatic writings are also echoed in the burgeoning field of holistic health and wellness. Here, the marriage of mind, body, and spirit is often likened to the Emerald Tablets' teachings, which emphasize balance and harmony in all aspects of life. Practitioners advocate for lifestyle choices that reflect the idea of microcosm and macrocosm, encouraging a synchronicity between personal well-being and environmental health.

Technological advancements have facilitated the spread of the Emerald Tablets' teachings, allowing digital platforms and online communities to explore their interpretations. These digital spaces provide a forum for global exchange and expansion of ideas. Practitioners and enthusiasts share insights and personal reflections, further weaving the Tablets' wisdom into the fabric of contemporary spirituality. Such interactions breathe new life into ancient teachings, making them accessible to a wider audience eager for authentic spiritual experiences.

Despite diverse interpretations, a common thread unites them: the Tablets are seen as a call for self-discovery and transformation. This perspective not only encourages a deeper understanding of oneself but also a greater awareness of one's connection to the universe. Thoth's teachings, as captured in the Emerald Tablets, challenge individuals to transcend the mundane and glimpse the divine—a pursuit that remains as relevant today as it was millennia ago.

Emerging from the shadows of antiquity, the Emerald Tablets continue to spark curiosity and exploration. They invite all seekers to engage with their messages in a way that resonates deeply with individual truth. This artistic freedom to interpret and adapt the Tablets is a testament to their enduring legacy, proving that though rooted in ancient tradition, the wisdom of the Emerald Tablets is eternally new—a compass guiding humanity towards a more enlightened future.

Impact on New Age Movements

In the heart of the 20th century, when society was hurtling towards technological advancement, a countercultural wave began to ripple through the consciousness of many. This wave was characterized by a return to ancient wisdom, a thirst for the sacred and mystical that seemed lost in the modern world. Central to this was the rediscovery of the Emerald Tablets, texts that resonated deeply with New Age Movements seeking spiritual enlightenment and transformation.

New Age Movements emerged as collectives of individuals and communities yearning for personal and spiritual growth. These groups sought knowledge that transcended conventional religious structures, looking towards ancient and mystical sources that offered deeper metaphysical insights. The Emerald Tablets, with their cryptic yet profound teachings attributed to Thoth, became a beacon for those on this quest. They offered a view of reality that was richly symbolic and philisophically potent, presenting life as an interconnected tapestry woven by invisible spiritual threads.

Many New Age adherents found the principles encapsulated within the Tablets, such as transmutation and the unity of all life, to be in harmony with the holistic and integrative approaches they championed. The notion of "as above, so below," directly linked to Hermetic thought, found its way into the core philosophies of New Age spirituality. This principle suggested that the microcosm and the macrocosm are reflections of one another, an idea that appealed to those seeking to understand their place within the universe.

The Tablets encouraged a personal journey of transformation akin to alchemical transmutation, which resonated with the New Age focus on personal growth and self-actualization. Individuals were drawn to the concept of evolving from base to noble forms, whether in character, spiritual understanding, or emotional healing. This transformative doctrine invited seekers to become modern-day alchemists, not through the manipulation of physical elements, but through the refinement of the self.

Notably, the teachings urged followers to explore the potential of the human mind and spirit, echoing the New Age's emphasis on expanding consciousness. Meditation, visualization, energy work, and other practices inspired by the Tablets became standard fare within New Age Circles. The Tablets' emphasis on balance and harmony with the cosmos encouraged individuals to align themselves not just spiritually, but physically and emotionally, with the world around them.

Moreover, the allegorical language of the Emerald Tablets inspired creative interpretations that fueled a diversity of practices and beliefs within the New Age movement. From crystal healing and energy medicine to psychic development and shamanic journeys, people interpreted the Tablets in ways that enriched their spiritual experiences. This flexibility and adaptability of interpretation allowed the Tablets to serve as a wellspring of inspiration across varying spiritual paths.

The expansive view of reality presented by the Tablets also contributed to a more inclusive spiritual perspective within New Age circles. The Tablets' teachings embraced a unity of all spiritual truths, aligning with the New Age tenet of syncretism—a blending of traditions from East and West, ancient and modern. Thoth's wisdom provided a common substrate, hinting at an underlying order amidst apparent chaos, encouraging adherents to seek the universality behind religious and mystical traditions.

Furthermore, the ecological consciousness central to many New Age ideologies found a sympathetic chord in the Emerald Tablets' emphasis on the interconnectedness of all life. The Tablets' allusions to cosmic law and natural order bolstered efforts to live harmoniously within the environment, driving initiatives rooted in sustainability and environmental stewardship. This idea of living in balance with the

Earth became pivotal, as adherents sought to manifest the Tablets' teachings in the form of practical ecological action.

As these esoteric ideas took root, the cultural and societal impact became more pronounced. The Emerald Tablets heavily influenced the literature and art of the New Age, inspiring films, music, and novels that explored mystical themes. These cultural artifacts, in turn, broadened the reach of the Tablets and their teachings, embedding these principles into the cultural fabric of the modern world.

The impact of the Emerald Tablets on New Age Movements highlights the enduring power of ancient wisdom to inspire, transform, and guide human consciousness. As seekers ponder these ancient writings, they're invited into a dialogue with time itself—echoes of a primordial consciousness that beckon the soul towards growth. Indeed, the Tablets' mystical allure continues to speak to the hearts of those yearning for spiritual illumination, adding to the ever-evolving tapestry of human understanding.

Chapter 8: Mystical Practices Influenced by the Tablets

In the quiet corners of history, away from the public gaze, ancient practices slipped into the hands of secret societies and devoted individuals. The Emerald Tablets, attributed to Thoth, became a cornerstone of these mystical pursuits. Those who sought to unlock their secrets delved into rituals that promised enlightenment and transformation. These practices were not mere repetitions of ancient techniques but evolved rituals infused with personal interpretations and modern understandings. Yet, they maintained a deep respect for the origins, providing insight into the cosmology and spirituality they represented.

The allure of the Tablets lay in their promise of transcendence, which inspired countless meditations developed over the ages. Practitioners believed these meditations could awaken inner wisdom and connect them to higher planes of existence. The focus often lay on aligning one's energies with the universe, reflecting the Hermetic principle, "As above, so below." Some techniques emphasized visualization and breathwork aimed at forming a direct connection with Thoth's wisdom, inviting seekers to transcend the mundane and embrace the divine.

Various esoteric schools and mystery traditions incorporated these mystical practices, adapting them to fit their unique philosophies while honoring the Tablets' core teachings. Initiates were encouraged to see themselves as both students and vessels of ancient knowledge—an alchemical journey known only to the few dedicated enough to pursue it. Case studies from different cultures reveal stories of individuals achieving profound insight and personal transformation through these practices, affirming their timeless relevance.

While the precise techniques varied, the essence of these mystical practices was universal: a pursuit of enlightenment, a harmonious balance between the material and spiritual realms, and an unwavering commitment to personal and spiritual growth. Connecting with the Emerald Tablets, steeped in their enigmatic teachings, offers a guiding light, leading seekers across the threshold of mystery and into the abode of wisdom.

Rituals and Meditations Linked to Thoth

Rituals and meditations inspired by the mystical teachings of Thoth offer unique pathways to connect with the wisdom of the Emerald Tablets. Thoth, often portrayed as a deity with the head of an ibis, symbolizes the intersection of the divine, the mystical, and the scholarly. His teachings, embedded within the Tablets, have inspired generations to explore the depths of consciousness. Many seekers have sought to recreate ancient practices purported to unlock hidden energies and enhance spiritual growth, echoing the profound harmonies depicted in these esoteric texts.

Some rituals connected to Thoth involve the chanting of sacred phrases, which are believed to resonate at specific frequencies that align with universal truths. Practitioners often engage in sound meditations alone or in groups, reciting passages attributed to the wisdom of Thoth to aid in their spiritual awakening. This auditory journey encourages participants to embark on a voyage through the layers of the subconscious mind, seeking clarity, transformation, and a deeper understanding of the universe. Such practices remind us that the Emerald Tablets are not just historical artifacts; they're dynamic guides to higher realities.

Meditation techniques linked to Thoth frequently incorporate visualization of light and geometry. Participants envision themselves bathed in emerald light, drawing power and insight from its ethereal glow. These visual meditations are said to open pathways to the akashic records, providing insights reserved for those willing to engage with Thoth's timeless teachings. By focusing on specific symbols associated with Thoth—like the ankh or the caduceus—practitioners claim to align themselves with the elemental forces of creation, fostering a sense of inner peace and cosmic understanding.

Through these rituals and meditations, followers of Thoth's wisdom strive to transcend ordinary perception. This blend of ancient and personalized practice serves not only as a testament to the enduring influence of the Emerald Tablets but also as a modern-day odyssey toward enlightenment. The path may be challenging, but the rewards of inner transformation and profound wisdom continue to inspire countless souls on their spiritual journeys.

Techniques to Unlock Thoth's Mystical Powers: The mystical allure of Thoth's teachings beckons seekers to journey beyond the veil of ordinary perception. Immersed in the lore of the Emerald Tablets, these techniques are more than mere rituals; they are gateways to profound transformation. Embedded within these practices is the essence of an ancient wisdom that whispers its secrets to those who dare to listen. Just as the ancient scribes of Egypt meticulously preserved Thoth's teachings, so too must modern practitioners approach these techniques with reverence and intention.

Core to the unlocking of Thoth's mystical powers is meditation, a timeless practice bridging the gap between the mundane and the divine. It's said that meditative states allow one to tune into Thoth's frequency, facilitating insights that transcend normal cognition. One common technique involves visualizing the Tablets themselves, allowing their imagery and inscriptions to guide one into deeper layers of understanding. The goal isn't merely to read the words but to let them resonate within, awakening dormant knowledge.

An additional meditative guidepost is the invocation of specific symbols associated with Thoth. This process can be likened to the Hermetic principle of Correspondence, where "As above, so below" becomes a transformative mantra. By aligning with these symbols, practitioners establish a connection with cosmic truths, prompting the soul's alignment with Thoth's wisdom. Envisioning the caduceus or Thoth's ibis helps ground the seeker in these mystical currents.

The power of sound, particularly the vibration of Thoth's name or resonant chants, plays a pivotal role in these practices. Sound has long been viewed as a sacred conduit for transformation in many traditions. Through repeated vocalization, practitioners can attune their energies to the universal frequency that Thoth embodies. In essence, such chants act as keys, unlocking mental doors guarding the inner sanctum of wisdom.

Rituals linked to lunar cycles provide a temporal framework for engaging with Thoth's teachings. The moon, closely associated with Thoth, magnifies the potential for spiritual work during key phases. New moons are ideal for setting intentions and beginning new practices, while full moons offer opportunities for revelation and clarity. Crafting rituals around these phases ensures that one's journey harmonizes with natural rhythms, amplifying the potency of Thoth's gifts.

Alchemical practices, inspired by Thoth's teachings, serve as both literal and metaphorical techniques for unlocking wisdom. While historical alchemists sought the transmutation of base metals into gold, spiritual alchemists view this as a metaphor for personal transformation. Approaching daily life with an alchemist's eye encourages the transmutation of negative patterns into life-affirming energies, thereby aligning one closer to the divine wisdom Thoth imparts.

Journals serve as practical tools for integrating Thoth's teachings into everyday life. Reflective writing, particularly following meditation or ritual, helps crystallize insights and track progress on the spiritual journey. Over time, these journals become a tapestry of personal growth, demonstrating how Thoth's ancient wisdom continues to unfold in contemporary contexts. Reviewing past entries reveals patterns and offers new revelations.

Dream work, too, is an invaluable technique in accessing Thoth's powers. Dreams often serve as gateways to subconscious realms where Thoth's teachings can manifest more vividly. Intentional dreaming, by keeping a dream journal or practicing lucid dreaming, can extend Thoth's influence into the subtle realms of consciousness. The ability to navigate dreams allows seekers to bring back insights that are both illuminating and transformative.

Group practices further expand the reach of Thoth's teachings. Gathering with others who are similarly aligned amplifies intentions and deepens the overall experience. Whether in formal circles or informal meetings, shared rituals, chants, and reflections create a collective energy that's often more potent than solitary endeavors. These gatherings honor the lineage of Thoth in a communal context, rekindling the ancient tradition of oral teaching and shared wisdom.

Visual art and creative expression form yet another avenue for unlocking Thoth's mystical powers. In ancient traditions, artistic creation was seen as a divine act that mirrored Thoth's role as a scribe of the gods. Modern seekers can engage with Thoth's essence through painting, drawing, or even dance, allowing the subconscious to express insights that defy verbalization. Creativity thus becomes a bridge, connecting the earthly with the ethereal.

Lastly, the act of service, often overlooked, stands as a powerful technique linked to Thoth's teachings. By committing oneself to serve others, practitioners embody the wisdom of Thoth through action. This selfless giving aligns with the universal truths that Thoth illuminates, ensuring that his teachings resonate not just within the individual but beyond, in the wider world.

In conclusion, unlocking Thoth's mystical powers is not a singular event but a continual process of alignment, exploration, and realization. These techniques, whether through meditation, ritual, sound, or service, open pathways to wisdom that echo through the ages. While the journey may begin with the self, its true culmination is in the interconnectedness of all beings, guided by the timeless truths of Thoth.

Case Studies of Successful Applications

The Emerald Tablets, steeped in mystery and ancient allure, have been a source of inspiration for mystics and seekers throughout history. Yet, what truly stands out in their legacy is how these arcane teachings have translated into actionable practices with profound impacts on individuals and communities. Across the globe, a series of fascinating case studies demonstrate how the Tablets' teachings have been applied successfully, shifting personal paradigms and influencing broader societal and spiritual movements.

One of the most compelling case studies comes from the heart of modern-day Egypt, where a spiritual community sought to revive ancient practices tied to Thoth's teachings. Utilizing rituals extracted from the translations of the Tablets, the group designed meditative techniques that mirrored the original rituals believed to have been practiced in the temple complexes of ancient Egypt. Participants reported enhanced states of awareness and spiritual connectivity, transcending the ordinary senses to tap into a higher realm of consciousness. These experiences underscore the enduring potential of Thoth's teachings to unlock latent human capabilities.

In another striking example, a group in the United States took inspiration from the Emerald Tablets to address the healing of emotional trauma. By integrating principles of transmutation—central to both the teachings of the Tablets and broader alchemical traditions—therapists introduced a novel approach to psychotherapy. Patients were guided to transform their emotional pain into narratives of strength and resilience, mirroring the Tablets' alchemical process of turning base metals into gold. This process not only facilitated recovery but also empowered individuals by linking their personal journeys to the timeless saga of transformation and rebirth.

Some distance away, on the secluded islands of the Pacific, a community-driven initiative embarked on a different yet equally transformative path. Drawing from the Tablets' insights on the interconnection of all life, they launched a conservation project that aimed to preserve their threatened natural habitat. Here, the principle of correspondence—"as above, so below"—guided their efforts. By recognizing the symbiotic relationship between human actions and environmental health, residents fostered a profound respect for nature. Their success in reviving ecosystems and restoring biodiversity stands as a testament to the profound ecological wisdom encapsulated within the Tablets.

In South America, an intriguing blend of shamanistic practices and Thoth's teachings took hold amidst the vibrant tapestry of Amazonian culture. Shamans, traditionally revered as custodians of spiritual and herbal knowledge, found in the Tablets a complementary framework for their rituals. By overlaying Thoth's principles with ancestral wisdom, they crafted healing ceremonies that addressed both spiritual and physical ailments. These ceremonies, believed to harness cosmic energies described in the Tablets, drew attendees from around the world, eager to experience personal transformation through this unique confluence of ancient traditions.

A notable case is found in the rise of new educational paradigms influenced by the Emerald Tablets. A progressive school in Europe, captivated by Thoth's depiction as the god of knowledge and writing, adopted a holistic curriculum inspired by the Tablets' teachings. They emphasized the integration of spiritual education alongside academic instruction, focusing on the development of wisdom as much as intellect. Students engaged in meditation and introspection exercises derived from interpretations of the Tablets, fostering a learning environment that nurtured both the mind and spirit. Over time, this approach led to remarkable transformations in students' critical thinking, empathy, and personal growth.

The modern business world has not remained untouched by these ancient teachings either. A pioneering management consultancy in

Asia applied principles from the Tablets to corporate strategy and leadership development. They emphasized the shaping of organizational culture through the lenses of alchemical transformation and hermetic balance, encouraging leaders to view their roles as alchemists, transforming organizational dynamics to achieve holistic success. The impact on company performance was tangible, underscoring how ancient wisdom can inform and enhance contemporary enterprise strategies.

Each of these case studies offers a glimpse into the multifaceted applications of the Emerald Tablets, bridging ancient wisdom and modern needs. They illustrate not only the adaptability of Thoth's teachings to diverse contexts but also their timeless relevance in addressing contemporary challenges. By weaving these ancient practices into the fabric of modern life, practitioners have unlocked pathways to personal and collective enlightenment, continuing the legacy of the Tablets as beacons of wisdom and transformation.

The success stories illustrate that the Tablets, with their mystical allure, hold a power far greater than historical curiosity. They are a living legacy, reshaping lives and communities beyond the boundaries of time and culture. Whether through meditation, healing, environmental stewardship, education, or business innovations, the essence captured within these ancient texts continues to shine, as vivid and vital as ever.

Chapter 9: The Scientific Perspective on the Tablets

Exploring the scientific perspective on the Emerald Tablets turns a mystical quest into a rigorous inquiry. The sheer antiquity of these enigmatic slabs calls for a balanced examination through the lens of history, archaeology, and textual analysis. In an era where science and spirituality often appear to diverge, the Tablets invite us to merge these avenues of thought, challenging our understanding of ancient wisdom.

The quest for historical validity is not merely about proving the existence of the Tablets but understanding their context within a broader scope of human civilization. Ancient texts, like the Dead Sea Scrolls or the Vedas, offer parallels and contrasts that illuminate the unique position of the Emerald Tablets. Such comparative analyses help us to grasp whether the teachings attributed to Thoth were borrowed, adapted, or entirely novel. This exercise of cross-examining ancient manuscripts allows modern scholars to see threads of interconnectedness across time, suggesting a shared wellspring of universal truths dispersed among varied cultures.

Examining the Tablets demands more than just historical comparison. Scientific analysis also covers the material composition of the Tablets—were they indeed crafted from a mythical "emerald" substance, or were they conventional in material yet divine in their narrative? Contemporary research methods, including spectrographic analysis and carbon dating, provide insights that ancient scribes might not have imagined. These methods help demystify the artifacts without diminishing their sacred value, allowing scholars and seekers alike to engage with both facts and faith.

What do scholars think about the influence of the Emerald Tablets? Opinions range broadly. Some view them as pivotal in the transmission of Hermetic knowledge, crucial to both Western and

Eastern esoteric traditions. Others perceive them as allegorical, serving as philosophical treatises that offer transcendent teachings rather than historical accounts. Dissecting these scholarly debates gives modern audiences a spectrum of interpretations to consider, urging readers to draw their conclusions from a well of diverse thought.

At the heart of these scientific endeavors lies an inspiring narrative that invites us to transcend the dichotomy of science and spirituality. The journey of the Emerald Tablets through time is not just about tracing their origins or confirming their authenticity. It's an exploration into how ancient wisdom can be reframed in a modern context, opening new doors to understanding. Scientists and historians may strive to reveal truths through data and facts, yet the Tablets continue to challenge assumptions, whispering secrets of the universe that defy empirical confines.

The intersection of the Emerald Tablets and science is a reflective passage—a reminder that we stand at the crossroads of two great traditions. Whether scrutinized under a microscope or read beneath a flickering candle, these Tablets compel us to ask questions. What realities lie behind the symbols? And how can this amalgam of ancient knowledge and contemporary insight guide us towards enlightenment? As the scientific journey unfolds, the Tablets remain a beacon, offering glimpses into a past that continues to shape our search for truth.

Investigating the Historical Validity

Throughout history, the Emerald Tablets have sparked fascination and debate among scholars, mystics, and seekers of ancient wisdom. Tracing the Tablets' historical authenticity is akin to peeling away layers of time, each revealing insights into the past yet shrouding them in further mystery. The quest to authenticate these enigmatic relics prompts us to question the intertwining paths of legend and recorded history—did myth become history, or did history birth the myth?

One approach to validating the Tablets is through the cross-examination of historical texts and archaeological data. Historians and archaeologists continuously endeavor to uncover evidence that either substantiates or refutes the Tablets' place in ancient history. Some argue that the absence of direct references in known ancient records casts doubt, while others point to indirect mentions and the pervasive influence of Thoth, the purported author, as indicators of their authenticity. This ongoing academic tug-of-war mirrors our intrinsic yearning to connect with the past in a tangible way.

The challenge lies not just in the scarcity of physical evidence but in deciphering the symbology and language that the Tablets encompass. Unlike straightforward historical manuscripts, the Tablets weave a narrative dense with metaphorical and alchemical symbolism. Discerning their historical context requires not only linguistic skill but a deep understanding of ancient cultural practices and philosophies. These elements combined draw an ambiguous yet captivating portrait of history that tempts curiosity and scholarly debate alike.

Despite these academic hurdles, the pursuit of historical validity continues to inspire contemporary scholars. As we delve deeper, each discovery or interpretation only serves to enhance our understanding of these ancient works. Understanding the Tablets' origins and purpose may forever remain elusive, yet the search itself enriches our journey through the corridors of time, drawing us ever closer to the profound mysteries they hold.

Comparative Analysis with Other Ancient Texts reflects a profound journey—not only through the lines of the Emerald Tablets but into the very heart of ancient wisdom. Our exploration begins with a critical examination of how these texts measure up against other hallowed ancient writings. It's a journey that seeks to uncover shared echoes of universal truths, weaving together the esoteric and the empirical.

In dissecting the historical validity of the Emerald Tablets, we dive into a rich tapestry of ancient literature. Comparable narratives emerge, stretching from the wisdom literature of ancient Egypt and Mesopotamia to the philosophical musings found in the Vedas and Upanishads of India. Each text, in its unique cultural and geographical context, seems to resonate with a similar frequency—the deep search for greater meaning and understanding of the cosmos.

Take the ancient Egyptian Book of the Dead, for instance. While primarily a funerary manuscript, its spells and incantations offer remarkable insights into life, death, and the afterlife. Parallels appear between its existential inquiries and those in the Emerald Tablets, with each exploring the soul's journey through metaphysical realms. There emerges an overarching narrative of transformation, not merely of the physical self but of spiritual transcendence—a theme that Thoth himself, the purported author of the Tablets, expertly spins throughout the texts.

Yet, Thoth is not alone in his teachings. Across the sands of time in ancient Mesopotamia, the Epic of Gilgamesh weaves a tale of human struggle against the immutable forces of nature and destiny. Here too, we see a profound quest for immortality, a pursuit that echoes within the alchemical roots of the Emerald Tablets. Understanding life's impermanence and the desire for eternal wisdom becomes a shared quest across cultures. These stories, though geographically distant, reveal humanity's undying thirst for knowledge and its transformative power.

The Upanishads, a significant component of Hindu sacred scriptures, offer another fascinating point of comparison. They delve into mysticism, metaphysics, and the essence of the self—ideas that resonate with the subtle teachings found within the Tablets. The concept of "Brahman," the ultimate reality beyond the illusory world, parallels Thoth's expressions of unity and divinity. Both sets of texts invite seekers to transcend the mundane and embrace a higher, more unified state of consciousness.

Moreover, the Hermetic Corpus—central to the development of Western esoteric thought—acknowledges the influence of Egyptian lore and the figure of Thoth. These Greek texts, with their profound explorations of divine truths, reflect an intellectual heritage shared with the Emerald Tablets. They convey hermetic principles, such as the Law of Correspondence, that are deeply intertwined with the ethos of the Tablets. It's an exchange of ideas bridging the ancient world's many cultural divides, creating a mosaic of shared insights.

As we sift through these ancient writings, it becomes evident that they serve as both mirrors and windows. They reflect the historical and cultural milieu of their creators while providing windows into universal human experiences and aspirations. The timeless search for meaning, the desire for spiritual ascension, and the quest for wisdom transcend the boundaries of time and place.

The Tao Te Ching, revered in Taoism, introduces yet another facet of this comparative analysis. It presents a worldview centered around harmony, balance, and the natural order—key ideas that resonate with the teachings inscribed in the Emerald Tablets. Just as the Tablets emphasize the balance of cosmic forces and inner alchemy, the Tao Te Ching urges an alignment with the Tao, the fundamental nature of the universe.

These ancient texts invite us into an intricate dance of ideas, with the Emerald Tablets at their core, spinning a tale that is at once unique and familiar. By comparing these texts, we unearth a shared narrative thread that underscores a fundamental human reality: the relentless pursuit of truth and enlightenment. Their wisdom, though often shrouded in mystery, remains a beacon for those who seek to unravel life's greatest mysteries.

Far from mere relics of the past, these texts stand as guideposts in a grand journey—a journey through the labyrinth of human consciousness, understanding, and spiritual evolution. Each tablet, each verse beckons us to delve deeper into the mysteries of life, urging us to reach beyond the known into the boundless realms of potential wisdom. Through a comparative exploration, we gain a broader perspective, one that infuses ancient teachings with renewed relevance for today's seekers of truth.

Scholarly Opinions on the Tablets' Influence

The Emerald Tablets, with their ethereal allure and mystic acumen, have long been a source of fascination and debate among scholars. While some see them as a treasure trove of esoteric wisdom, others question their origins and impacts. This section delves into the varied scholarly opinions that paint a complex picture of the Tablets' influence on historical and contemporary thought.

From the outset, many scholars have been drawn to the Tablets' cryptic language and profound themes. These ancient artifacts, attributed to the mythical figure Thoth, display an enigma that scholars like to unravel. Academic circles often regard the Tablets as a sophisticated metaphorical system that conceals layers of understanding beneath the surface. The intricate use of metaphors and symbols invites continuous interpretation, challenging scholars to delve deeper into the nuanced layers of meaning.

There's a consensus that the influence of the Tablets extends beyond their historical context, touching upon the philosophical and spiritual realms. Scholars argue that the core teachings of the Tablets encapsulate universal truths that resonate with many ancient wisdom traditions. These timeless principles, coupled with the mythical stature of Thoth, fuel academic exploration into the intertwining of esoteric knowledge and empirical investigation.

One notable scholarly stance posits that the Emerald Tablets served as a catalyst for the emergence of hermeticism. This philosophical and religious system, which flourished during the late antiquity, bears testament to the profound impact of the Tablets. By examining historical connections, researchers suggest that the Tablets' teachings permeated through to Hermes Trismegistus' writings, further influencing Hermetic thought. This relationship highlights the Tablets' role in shaping intellectual paradigms throughout history.

However, amidst this admiration, skepticism has also found its place. Some critics contend that the Tablets are not genuine relics of an ancient civilization, but rather, a medieval construct borne from alchemical symbolism. This critical viewpoint emphasizes the need for a circumspect interpretation of the Tablets, urging scholars to assess the possibility of later additions or reinterpretations that have colored their perceived influence.

Others advocate for a balanced perspective, acknowledging the blend of historical truths and legendary embellishments. By comparing the Tablets with other ancient texts, such as the Corpus Hermeticum or the Nag Hammadi library, scholars can gain insights into the cultural and historical milieu in which these writings were conceived. Such comparative analyses provide a more grounded understanding and illuminate the interconnectedness of various knowledge systems across different epochs.

Recent scholarly work has also explored the enduring relevance of the Emerald Tablets within contemporary spiritual and philosophical environments. Scholars assert that the Tablets possess a remarkable ability to transcend specific temporal and geographical contexts, thus inviting a myriad of modern interpretations and adaptations. This timeless appeal might explain why so many seekers of truth continue to explore the Tablets' contents, incorporating them into current spiritual movements such as New Ageism.

Moreover, interdisciplinary collaborations between scholars and practitioners of mystic and spiritual traditions reveal the Tablets' dynamic role in modern times. By bridging academic inquiry with pragmatic applications, scholars illuminate the ongoing legacy of the Tablets in spiritual and self-development practices. It becomes evident that the Tablets' influence extends not only to historical scholarship but also infuses contemporary paths toward personal and collective enlightenment.

The discourse surrounding the Tablets is enriched by debates over their linguistic characteristics. Experts dissect the original language, suggesting that its deliberate ambiguity serves as both a challenge and an invitation to dive deep into the interpretative process. This linguistic complexity creates a perennial ground for scholarly debate, encouraging an endless pursuit of deciphering the Tablets' intended wisdom.

As scholarship continues to evolve, the dialogue around the Emerald Tablets remains vibrant, driven by the ongoing quest to understand their true origins and meaning. Despite varying perspectives, there's a shared recognition of the Tablets' role as a conduit for wisdom that balances esoteric mystique with philosophical depth. Scholars, thus, find themselves perpetually captivated by the enigmatic glow of the Emerald Tablets, pondering their mysteries and celebrating their enduring influence on the tapestry of human thought.

Chapter 10: Thoth's Wisdom Across Cultures

As we journey further into the rich tapestry of Thoth's teachings, we find ourselves at the crossroads of various cultures, each uniquely interpreting the wisdom imparted by the legendary Egyptian deity. Thoth, often regarded as the scribe of the gods and the patron of knowledge, has inspired a wealth of interpretations spanning ancient civilizations. As we explore the breadth of his impact, we begin to see how his principles have woven themselves into the fabric of cultural narratives across the world.

The reverberations of Thoth's wisdom are not confined to the boundaries of Egypt. Ancient Greece revered him as Hermes Trismegistus, a syncretic fusion of the Egyptian god and their own messenger deity, Hermes. This amalgamation gave birth to Hermeticism, a system of thought that sought to unlock the mysteries of the universe through spiritual and philosophical exploration. The Greeks, forever seekers of knowledge, found a kindred spirit in Thoth whose teachings aligned with their quest for enlightenment through reason and introspection.

Similarly, in ancient Mesopotamia, there are parallels to be found between Thoth and Nabu, the god of wisdom and writing. Both deities were closely linked to the development of writing systems and the preservation of knowledge. While distinct in their own right, Nabu's traits reflected the reverence accorded to Thoth and his emphasis on the transformative power of education and the written word. This connection underscores the shared understanding of divine wisdom transcending cultural boundaries.

Venture further east, and you'll find echoes of Thoth in India's Vedic traditions. Thoth's essence resonates with Brihaspati, the sage of the gods, who similarly embodies wisdom and eloquence. The Indian subcontinent, with its rich philosophical traditions, draws subtle connections between these divine figures, emphasizing how the pursuit of wisdom is a universal endeavor. The reflective nature of their teachings urges us to seek knowledge not as an accumulation of facts but as a deeper understanding of our interconnected existence.

In the Far East, Taoist thought mirrors many of Thoth's teachings, particularly in its appreciation for balance and harmony. Thoth's wisdom often touches upon the cosmic principles of order and chaos, a theme that resonates within the yin-yang philosophy. Both paradigms suggest that true wisdom lies in recognizing and harmonizing these opposing forces within ourselves and the world around us. The dialogue between Thoth's ideas and Eastern philosophies illustrates a shared yearning for equilibrium in human endeavors.

The adaptation of Thoth's wisdom into various cultural contexts showcases not only the fluidity of his teachings but also their fundamental relevance. As these civilizations absorbed and reinterpreted Thoth's messages, they offered their own perspectives on the ancient truths contained within the Emerald Tablets. This nuanced process of cultural integration demonstrates the timelessness of Thoth's insights, capable of informing diverse philosophical discourses.

In Mesoamerican cultures, gods resembling Thoth appear within their pantheon, embodying similar attributes of communication and intellect. Though geographically distant, the appreciation for divine wisdom and its human intermediaries appears as a common thread. This global tapestry of interpretations suggests that Thoth's influence is not limited to any one tradition but is instead a universal exploration of human consciousness and its origins.

A cross-cultural analysis of Thoth's teachings reveals a profound interconnectedness among ancient civilizations in their quest to comprehend the divine. Each culture, while distinct in its interpretation, shares a reverence for wisdom as a guiding principle. By examining these cultural convergences, we gain insight into how

Thoth's legacy continues to inspire and shape our understanding of ourselves and the cosmos.

As we reflect on Thoth's global journey through history, we're reminded of the power of wisdom to transcend cultural and temporal divides. In our modern quest for understanding, Thoth's teachings encourage us to explore a synthesis of ancient knowledge and contemporary thought. The challenge, perhaps, is to take these timeless lessons and apply them to the challenges of today, crafting a narrative that continues to honor the past while embracing the future. Thus, Thoth's wisdom thrives, ever expanding and evolving across the ages.

Cross-Cultural Interpretations and Beliefs

Thoth, known as the scribe of the gods in ancient Egyptian culture, casts a long shadow across diverse civilizations. His wisdom is akin to a universal language, transcending time and geography, inviting myriad interpretations and beliefs. Thoth's principles, encapsulated in the Emerald Tablets, resonate with esoteric traditions worldwide, creating a web of mystical dialogue that spans continents. This section delves into how various cultures have interpreted Thoth's teachings, each adding their own layers of meaning.

In ancient Greece, Thoth was syncretized with Hermes Trismegistus, a composite figure embodying wisdom and magic. The Greeks, renowned for their intellectual pursuits, found in Hermes a patriarch of philosophy and science, drawing parallels between Thoth's teachings and their burgeoning intellectual traditions. Ancient Greek philosophers saw the Emerald Tablets as a key to understanding the mysteries of the natural world and the cosmos. They regarded Thoth's wisdom as a cornerstone in the construction of Hermetic Philosophy, impacting their metaphysical explorations and spiritual practices.

As we journey further east, echoes of Thoth's teachings appear in Indian spiritual texts. Elements of the Tablets resonate with Vedic and Upanishadic writings, where the eternal flow of wisdom and knowledge is revered. The cyclical nature of creation, preservation, and destruction depicted in these texts finds a mirror in Thoth's teachings of transformation and transmutation. Here, Thoth's influence isn't viewed through a literal lens but rather as an archetypal embodiment of profound spiritual knowledge.

In the expansive sands of Arabia, Thoth found expression in the teachings of Islamic alchemists. During the Islamic Golden Age, scholars and mystics explored the syncretic link between Thoth's wisdom and Islamic science. They embarked on quests to uncover the hidden truths of the natural world, employing Thoth's teachings as a foundation for alchemical and philosophical inquiry. The Emerald Tablets, translated into Arabic, infused their pursuit of knowledge with both divine inspiration and empirical investigation, blending the metaphysical with the material.

Meanwhile, in Mesoamerica, Thoth's wisdom echoes in the teachings of the ancient Mayans and Aztecs. Though there is no direct line of transmission, symbolic parallels can be drawn between Thoth's teachings and the intricate calendars and cosmology of these cultures. Their understanding of time, cycles, and celestial movements reflects Thoth's influence on human consciousness, as they too sought to align earthly life with the divine order of the universe.

Today, the comprehensive embrace of Thoth across cultures reveals a profound truth: the quest for understanding and enlightenment is a shared human journey. Each cultural interpretation of Thoth's teachings offers a unique perspective, enriching the global tapestry of wisdom. As seekers of ancient knowledge, we inherit this legacy, drawn to the universal truths that reverberate within the Emerald Tablets. In exploring these cross-cultural interpretations, we find not only echoes of distant civilizations but also insights that continue to inform our spiritual evolution, awakening a deeper connection to the mystical dimensions of our shared existence.

Similarities with Other Ancient Civilizations can be as fascinating as they are illuminating, offering a glimpse into the shared consciousness of early humanity. Let's delve into the profound connections between Thoth's teachings within the Emerald Tablets and the philosophical and spiritual structures of other ancient cultures. These connections are neither random nor superficial. Instead, they highlight a universal quest for understanding the nature of existence and the mysteries of life.

We start with a civilization known for its ordered society and prodigious contributions to philosophy and science: Ancient Greece. The reverence for Thoth in Egyptian culture as the deity of wisdom, writing, and mathematics finds echoes in the Greek god Hermes. In fact, Hermes Trismegistus, a syncretic figure who emerged much later, is believed to be a blending of Thoth and Hermes, linking Egyptian and Greek traditions in the shared search for knowledge. This symbolizes a philosophical bridge between these two ancient cultures, highlighting the universality of these pursuits across geographic and cultural boundaries.

Moving eastward to the ancient civilizations of Mesopotamia, we find echoes of Thoth's wisdom in the Assyrian and Babylonian practices. The Emerald Tablets' teachings on alchemy and transformation resonate with the Mesopotamian understanding of life and death cycles and their fascination with medicinal plants and metals. These cultures held a belief in an interconnected universe, much like the Hermetic principle of correspondence, which finds its roots in Thoth's philosophy. Such parallels suggest a cross-pollination of ideas revolving around sacred science that spans diverse lands and epochs.

One can't overlook the striking similarities between Thoth's writings and the ancient Vedic texts from India. Themes of transformation and divine wisdom prevalent in the Emerald Tablets align with the Vedic emphasis on spiritual elevation and the pursuit of universal truth. Just as Thoth is depicted as a transcriber of divine knowledge, the god Brahma in Hinduism represents the ultimate creator and the sacred scriptures, the Vedas, are regarded as repositories of universal wisdom.

Moreover, the concept of cosmic harmony that runs through the Emerald Tablets is mirrored in the Taoist philosophies of ancient China. The Emerald Tablets speak of an order and balance inherent in all things, reminiscent of the Taoist principles of Yin and Yang, and the quest for harmony with the Tao, or the Way. Both emphasize the importance of aligning with the cosmos, recognizing a profound, subtle order that governs life.

Cross-cultural examination also brings to light interesting connections between early Mesoamerican civilizations and the teachings attributed to Thoth. The feathered serpent god, Quetzalcoatl, revered in Aztec and Toltec traditions, shares characteristics with Thoth. Both are associated with creation, wisdom, and the stars, underlining a shared archetypal symbol of knowledge and spiritual enlightenment that transcends different worldviews.

Exploring similarities with the ancient civilizations of the Celts in Europe, we notice a fascinating intersection of sacred traditions and metaphysical thought. Their oral tradition, with an emphasis on the power of words and the spoken spell, resonates with Thoth's association with writing and magic. It showcases a form of ancient wisdom where language was seen as a tool of creation and transformation, much as Thoth is portrayed within the Egyptian pantheon.

These extensive cross-cultural threads reflect a universal drive towards wisdom and enlightenment, forming an intricate tapestry of human thought. It's as if different cultures drank from the same wellspring of knowledge, albeit through unique lenses molded by their distinct environments and needs. This demonstrates not only the resilience of certain themes across time and space but also the inherent human desire to seek understanding of the great mysteries of life.

The global convergence of ancient wisdom as seen through the prism of Thoth's teachings provides an inspirational narrative for modern-day seekers. It emphasizes that while methods and symbols may differ, the essence of seeking truth and knowledge spans across cultures, drawing humanity together in a shared journey through the annals of time. This view invites us to appreciate and learn from historical interconnections, reminding us that the quest for wisdom is a shared heritage, cultivated and refined across generations and continents.

As we delve deeper into the Emerald Tablets, it is essential to recognize these similarities not as mere coincidences but as evidence of a profound interplay and dialogue between ancient civilizations. Each brought forth its own unique contributions yet participated in a universal tapestry of wisdom that, to this day, continues to inspire and guide the quest for understanding within contemporary spirituality and thought.

Cultural Adaptations and Integrations

As we traverse the vast landscape of Thoth's wisdom, one can't help but notice the myriad ways it has woven itself into the cultural tapestries around the world. Each society, with its unique context and understanding, has adapted and integrated the wisdom of the Emerald Tablets in ways that resonate with its own values and cosmology. This chapter seeks to explore these cultural adaptations, shedding light on how the Tablets' teachings transcended their Egyptian origins to influence a global paradigm.

Many stunning examples exist where the spiritual insights from the Emerald Tablets were woven into the fabric of other cultures, each integration as unique as the civilization that embraced it. In ancient Greece, the synthesis of Egyptian knowledge with Greek philosophy gave birth to Hellenistic Hermeticism, an evolving spiritual system that projected Thoth's teachings into the heart of Western thought. The resulting blend was a rich alchemical mix of ideas, including notions of nature's unity and the divine knowledge embedded in the cosmos.

India, with its deep mystical traditions, offers another perspective on how Thoth's timeless wisdom found a voice in new cultural landscapes. The concept of transforming base metals into gold can easily parallel the Siddhis, or mystical achievements, described in ancient Vedic texts. This transformation, a cornerstone of both Indian and Egyptian philosophical teachings, speaks to universal truths that transcend geography.

A fascinating cross-cultural nod to the influence of the Emerald Tablets can be seen in the amalgamation of wisdom traditions in the Islamic world during the medieval period. Scholars in the House of Wisdom in Baghdad voraciously translated and preserved ancient texts, including those attributed to Hermes Trismegistus, the Graeco-Egyptian version of Thoth. This synthesis of ideas helped shape the intellectual landscape of the Islamic Golden Age, influencing disciplines such as alchemy and astrology, all the while intertwining with Thoth's insights.

African indigenous cultures too embraced and morphed the esoteric teachings of Thoth. Here, the Tablets resonated with long-standing traditions that viewed the world as alive with spiritual forces. The ritualistic aspects of Thoth's wisdom found echoes in African spiritual practices, such as those involving the communication with ancestors and spirits, and the understanding of the earth's cycles.

Moving into East Asia, one can discern parallels between the ideas of balance and duality found within the Emerald Tablets and those pervasive in Daoist philosophy. Concepts such as the harmonizing of opposites and the pursuit of spiritual immortality reflect the Tao, emphasizing a universal congruence that underlies different cultural interpretations of similar metaphysical principles.

Furthermore, in the Americas, traditional Mayan and Incan philosophies revered deities of knowledge and wisdom similar to Thoth, valuing the sacred geometry and cosmic order that the Emerald Tablets espoused. These civilizations created intricate calendars and cosmologies that mirror Thoth's teachings on cosmic cycles.

Even into the modern era, the wisdom of the Emerald Tablets continues to find expression in ways that resonate with contemporary cultural movements. The rise of global spirituality in the 20th and 21st centuries has seen these ancient teachings re-emerge, adapted for today's seekers. Many spiritual communities worldwide have taken up the mantle of Thoth's teachings, using them as a bridge between ancient wisdom and present-day enlightenment pursuits.

The integration of Thoth's wisdom into different cultures demonstrates a dynamic process where ideas evolve and adapt to new settings. This perpetual adaptation underscores the universality of these teachings, proving that they are not bound by time or place. They speak to an inner truth that transcends borders, resonating with the quest for understanding and enlightenment at the heart of the human experience.

Cultural adaptation isn't merely a matter of passive acceptance; it involves active integration, where Thoth's teachings are interwoven with local traditions and worldviews. This process has enriched not only the cultures that have embraced these teachings but also the teachings themselves, as each new interpretation brings fresh insights and renewed relevance.

Understanding these cultural adaptations allows us to appreciate the diverse manifestations of wisdom across the globe, whilst acknowledging a shared lineage of thought that binds us all in our collective history. It invites us to recognize the importance of cultural exchange in the continuing evolution of spiritual wisdom.

Reflecting on these adaptations challenges us to consider the essence of Thoth's wisdom. How can we, in our unique cultural milieus, authentically engage with these teachings to enrich our understanding of ourselves and the universe around us? This reflection not only enriches our grasp of the past but also empowers us to envision a future where ancient wisdom continues to inspire and guide contemporary seekers.

In the tapestry of human understanding, the threads of Thoth's wisdom provide a continuous line that connects and enriches diverse cultures, encouraging a dialogue that spans centuries. By tracing these lines, we gain perspective on the complex interplay between tradition and transformation that defines our spiritual histories.

Chapter 11: Unlocking the Secrets: Interpretative Challenges

The Emerald Tablets, steeped in mystique and shrouded in layers of cryptic language, have always posed a profound interpretative challenge. Scholars, spiritual seekers, and mystics alike have approached these ancient texts with a blend of reverence and curiosity, each hoping to extract nuggets of timeless wisdom relevant to their own contexts. These enigmatic pathways of knowledge invite us to delve deeper, to understand not just with the mind, but with the heart and spirit.

Over the centuries, interpretations of the Emerald Tablets have evolved significantly. What one era might have seen as literal truth, another regarded as metaphor or allegory. The tablets' ability to resonate uniquely with individuals across time underscores their extraordinary adaptability. However, this adaptability also begets complexity. Diverse readings and the myriad of interpretations have led to endless debates about their true meaning and purpose.

One reason for the varied interpretations is the tablets' symbolic language. Symbols act as gateways to understanding, yet they remain fluid, shifting forms according to the interpreter's perspective and cultural context. In this light, each interpretation becomes a reflection of the interpreter more than the text itself. This dynamic interplay between text and reader creates an evolving spectrum of understanding, where new insights emerge with each fresh perspective.

Furthermore, the historical context in which the tablets were written and subsequently discovered plays a crucial role. Originally, these teachings might have been intended for a select group of initiates, possessing the requisite knowledge to decipher their hidden messages. In the hands of a broader audience throughout history, these texts took on new dimensions, layered with additional meanings and woven into the philosophical and religious tapestries of diverse cultures.

Debates among scholars and mystics often revolve around the authorial intent. Some argue for a practical, alchemical interpretation, asserting that the tablets contain literal secrets of material transmutation. Others view them as purely metaphorical, pointing toward spiritual transformation and enlightenment. The ongoing discourse between these perspectives illustrates the richness and depth of the tablets' teachings and their ability to inspire varied paths to understanding.

This spectrum of interpretations is not without its challenges. Ambiguities within the text often lead to contradictions, even within single interpretations, which can be disconcerting for those seeking definitive answers. Yet, it's precisely this elusive nature that proves to be the tablets' greatest strength. It beckons to each reader, offering a personalized journey into the mysteries they hold, encouraging introspection and personal growth.

Understanding the Emerald Tablets also requires a readiness to embrace both intellect and intuition. A purely analytical approach risks missing the sublime nuances hidden within the text. Conversely, an approach grounded solely in mysticism may overlook the practical wisdom embedded within their verses. The key to unlocking these secrets lies in harmonizing these approaches, allowing the mind to question while the heart explores.

Personal reflection, therefore, becomes an essential part of engaging with the Emerald Tablets. Each seeker, armed with their own life experiences and worldviews, adds to the tapestry of interpretation. In doing so, they not only uncover the tablets' wisdom but also learn something about themselves, experiencing the profound connection between ancient teachings and contemporary life.

Ultimately, the challenge of interpretation offers an opportunity. It invites us to become active participants in the dance of understanding, encouraging us to remain open to new insights and perspectives. Through this process, we not only unlock the secrets of the Emerald

Tablets but also advance our personal quests for knowledge and meaning.

As we continue to engage with these ancient texts, let us approach them with humility and openness, understanding that while we may never fully unravel all their secrets, the journey of discovery is itself a noble pursuit. The tablets teach us that the search for truth is ongoing, an ever-unfolding process that challenges, enriches, and ultimately transforms us.

Diverse Interpretations Over Time

The saga of the Emerald Tablets extends far beyond their initial creation, offering a rich tapestry of interpretations that have evolved across centuries. These ancient texts, attributed to the enigmatic Hermes Trismegistus, known also as Thoth, continue to captivate minds eager to unravel their secrets. Over time, scholars, mystics, and seekers alike have engaged in vibrant debate about the Tablets' meanings, each group adding its own hue to the mosaic of understanding.

In the early centuries, when the Tablets first emerged in the consciousness of scholars, interpretations leaned heavily on their alchemical promises. Alchemy, with its tantalizing pursuit of the philosopher's stone and the transmutation of base metals into gold, found a kindred spirit in the Tablets. Scholars of the past were often torn between a literal and a symbolic reading, with some steadfastly convinced of their physical alchemical powers while others saw them as allegorical, revealing secrets of spiritual transformation.

As time advanced into the Middle Ages, the Emerald Tablets were cloaked in a veil of secrecy, largely due to the esoteric nature of their teachings. This period fostered a range of interpretations, from mystical to scientific, reflecting the era's intricate interplay between religion and burgeoning scientific inquiry. Interpretations during this time often mirrored the cultural tensions between the known and the unknown, the explainable and the mystical.

The Renaissance bloomed as a pivotal era for reinterpretation, as the Tablets were rediscovered and revered in new light. Influenced significantly by Hermeticism, the era saw a revival in the interest of ancient wisdom, intertwining with the emerging values of humanism and inquiry. Here, the Tablets' teachings were not just about the physical world but also pointed toward a holistic understanding of man and cosmos. This period's thinkers viewed the Tablets as keys to unlocking both scientific and metaphysical mysteries, a duality that opened new paths of exploration.

Fast forward to the modern era, and we encounter even more diverse interpretations, reflecting the dynamic shifts in spiritual and philosophical landscapes. In the wake of scientific rigidity and the rise of materialism, a resurgence in interest towards these ancient texts is notable. Interpretations now often focus on personal empowerment and spiritual awakening, aiming to bridge ancient insights with contemporary self-discovery movements. The New Age seekers interpret the Tablets' timeless wisdom as guidance for personal transformation and transcendence, finding relevance in its age-old allegories.

This ongoing evolution of interpretation underscores the complexity and depth of the Emerald Tablets. Each era, with its distinct frame of reference, sheds new light on their enigmatic teachings, ensuring that these ancient relics of wisdom continue to inspire and challenge. What stands out amidst the breadth of interpretations is how each generation finds within the Tablets a reflection of its own quests and aspirations. Indeed, the magic of the Emerald Tablets lies not just in their teachings but in their ability to stay relevant, forever morphing and adapting to the needs of those who seek their secrets.

Debates Among Scholars and Mystics have long stirred the waters of esoteric thinking, dousing the curious mind with questions rather than answers. Among these debates are profound discussions that pierce the veils of time and truth, centered on the Emerald Tablets. Throughout history, both scholars and mystics have ventured into the labyrinth of interpretations, each offering unique perspectives that range from the terrestrial to the divine. These conversations aren't mere academic exercises; they possess a vitality that speaks to the soul, inviting a deeper understanding of Thoth's wisdom. They reflect human nature's relentless quest to unravel the secrets of the cosmos and our place within it.

The diversity of opinions surrounding the Tablets is as ancient as their mythological origins. Consider the various interpretations debated over centuries: Are the Tablets purely allegorical, meant to provide metaphysical insights? Or do they hold literal truths that beckon us towards mystical experiences? These questions form a core part of the dialectic dance between scholarly critique and spiritual exploration. For scholars, the focus often lands on historical context and linguistic precision, sifting through ancient languages like miners panning for gold. Mystics, however, perceive the text as a living document, whose true meaning expands and shifts with the reader's spiritual evolution.

Historical scholars often approach the Tablets with a lens of critical analysis, grounding interpretations in the cultural and religious framework of early civilizations. They explore how the ancient Egyptian worldview, particularly its cosmology and deific hierarchies, can clarify the cryptic passages of the Tablets. Academic inquiry can bring structure and rigor to our understandings, offering pathways to unlock the layers of meaning embedded in the text. However, these often stark, precise analyses can be seen as limiting by those who seek experiential understanding.

Mystics, meanwhile, draw from a wellspring of personal insight and revelation. For many, the Tablets are not historical artifacts but living, breathing guides to spiritual ascension. They claim the texts contain a code, a vibrational language that communicates directly with the soul, bypassing the analytical mind. Such spiritual readings of the Tablets are less concerned with exact translations and more focused on the alchemical transformation of the reader, a transcendence that aligns with the teachings of Thoth himself.

Throughout time, these debates have been significantly influenced by shifting societal values and advancements in collective understanding. In the Middle Ages, for instance, the translation of the Emerald Tablets opened the door for their integration into Hermetic traditions, sparking a significant movement geared towards personal and spiritual enlightenment. Schools of thought like alchemy took particular interest in understanding the nature of transformation, both material and spiritual, as posited by the Tablets. This period saw a symbiotic relationship between scholarly critique and mystical practice.

The Renaissance brought its own brand of debate, as humanist scholars began to reconcile reason with mysticism. Increasing access to ancient texts allowed for comparative studies with newly discovered manuscripts from other cultures. Thinkers and seekers attempted to harmonize the wisdom of Thoth with seemingly disparate philosophies, aiming to uncover universal truths. This era of intellectual cross-pollination saw an intensifying of dialogue as the mystics' experiences were increasingly subjected to scholarly scrutiny.

In modern times, with the advent of technology and global communication, the debate over the Emerald Tablets finds new life. The digital age invites more voices into the discussion, transcending geographical and cultural barriers. Online forums and digital publications allow mystics, scholars, and enthusiasts alike to share insights, fostering a vibrant community of interpreters. Yet, with this increased accessibility comes new challenges, as distinguishing credible interpretations from those born of misinformation becomes a task of its own.

Many contemporary scholars argue that despite centuries of study, the true understanding of the Tablets remains elusive. This humility in the face of ancient wisdom poses an interesting juxtaposition to the certainty often projected by modern scientific inquiry. Unlike tangible artifacts, the words of the Emerald Tablets are ethereal in nature, their meaning seemingly dependent on the consciousness of the reader. As such, debates continue to oscillate between seeing them as magnificent metaphors or as esoteric roadmaps to enlightened states of being.

The mystics hold fast to the conviction that the Tablets serve as a mirror to the soul's journey. Whether through meditation, ritual practice, or sheer intuition, they pursue insight that transcends intellectual bindings. Their interpretations, often rich in symbolic depth, reveal pathways through which individuals can ascend toward higher states of consciousness. This quest for spiritual insight and ultimate unity with the divine characteristics of the Hermetic tradition is echoed through countless mystical practices worldwide.

These ongoing debates among scholars and mystics aren't mere conflicts; they are necessary for the vitality and dynamism of the study of the Emerald Tablets. They compel each generation to revisit and reinterpret Thoth's wisdom, ensuring it remains ever-relevant. As seekers of ancient wisdom, we are invited not only to explore these conversations but to engage with them. We are encouraged to question and to contemplate, to honor tradition while remaining open to revelation. As the Tablets themselves suggest, all truth is but a half-truth, leaving us always grasping toward an understanding just beyond our reach.

Thus, the tension between scholarship and mysticism creates a fertile ground for discoveries yet to come. It is within this interplay that the Emerald Tablets retain their mystique and power, constantly challenging us to look beyond the visible and into the realms of possibility. In doing so, we might move closer to unraveling the profound mysteries that have captivated human thought for millennia, the very mysteries we, as seekers, are driven to explore and comprehend.

Personal Reflection and Understanding

As we delve into the myriad interpretations and debates surrounding the Emerald Tablets, it becomes clear that this ancient text holds a special fascination, inviting not only scholarly analysis but also deep personal reflection. For those of us who seek a connection with ancient wisdom, the pursuit often leads to introspection, seeking to align external knowledge with inner understanding. This part of the journey might be just as transformational as understanding the text itself.

In grappling with the enigmatic teachings, we're compelled to consider our beliefs and worldviews. Many of us come to this exploration with preconceived notions, molded by our cultural and educational backgrounds. Yet, the Tablets challenge us to open our minds and hearts anew, to perceive reality through the lens of Thoth, a figure who embodies the balance between the mystical and the rational. This balance can lead us to moments of profound clarity, where intuition guides us just as strongly as intellect.

For me, the journey through the Tablets begins as a quest for outer knowledge but inevitably turns inward. Each line, steeped in symbolism, beckons me to pause, reflect, and listen to the echoes of ancient wisdom that subtly speak to my present self. The text acts as a mirror, reflecting not only the historical and mystical past but also the contours of my soul and the direction of my path. It's a reminder that ancient teachings are not static relics; they're living documents that resonate uniquely with each individual's life journey.

The challenge lies in unraveling the layered meanings embedded within the text. To approach this, I've often found it helpful to remember that understanding isn't a solitary act. It's a dialog with the centuries, with those who've sought before me, and with my own evolving sense of self. These dialogues are not only intellectual but are an emotional voyage where doubt and certainty, mystery and revelation intertwine.

Upon deeper reflection, one can't help but question the notion of "truth" as something singular and accessible. In the context of the Emerald Tablets, truth seems a mosaic of insights, experiences, and interpretations. What rings true for one may be merely a stepping stone for another. Thus, the Tablets serve less as answers carved in stone and more as invitations to embark upon a personal odyssey of discovery and understanding.

As seekers, we yearn for teachings that can transform our lives and align us more closely with universal truths. In my exploration, the most enlightening revelations have come not from dissecting every word but rather from letting go of the need to control the meaning. Instead, I've discovered that allowing the teachings to resonate on an instinctual level often reveals more than any logical analysis could. There's a kind of magic that happens when we let the words of the Tablets breathe through us, inviting patterns and synchronicities into our lives.

Sometimes, the most profound understandings arise not from intense study but through a casual encounter with an idea that nudges the subconscious. In a sudden flash of realization, it's as if a veil lifts, offering us a glimpse into a higher state of awareness that feels both deeply familiar and utterly new. These moments remind us that growth doesn't always follow the straight path of linear logic but often takes the winding trail of intuition and unexpected insight.

This reflective pursuit transforms the Tablets from a historical curiosity into a living wisdom, potent and relevant to the modern seeker. As I continue to engage with these texts, my understanding evolves, colored by the continuous flow of life's experiences and my own changing perspective.

The individual journey with the Emerald Tablets not only expands our minds but enriches our spiritual lives. It leads us to places within ourselves we might not have discovered otherwise, urging us toward a more thoughtful, compassionate, and interconnected existence. Such teachings underscore the timeless relevance of the Tablets.

Understanding these documents also involves embracing the paradoxes they present. The Tablets offer ideas that sometimes contradict and challenge our understanding of duality and unity, earthly life and cosmic existence. This paradox serves not to confuse but to expand our capacity to hold multiple truths simultaneously, transcending the dichotomy our minds often settle into. Indeed, the Tablets teach us that embracing complexity is key to unlocking not only their secrets but those within ourselves.

Ultimately, our personal reflections on the Tablets touch upon a central tenet of many wisdom traditions: the journey toward self-awareness and enlightenment is lifelong and continuous. There is no final chapter of learning. Each encounter with the Emerald Tablets returns us to a state of wonder, teaching us to ask not just "What do these words mean?" but also, "What do they mean to me, here and now?"

As I reflect on this enduring journey, it isn't merely about accumulating knowledge; it's about transforming that knowledge into wisdom that speaks directly to my life. In this way, the Emerald Tablets become not only ancient texts but living guides through the challenges and mysteries of life, offering unfathomable depth to those who seek it earnestly.

In this personal dance with the Emerald Tablets, I find myself constantly rejuvenated, driven to explore further both the inner landscapes of my being and the vast, mysterious landscapes offered by ancient wisdom. Through each reading, each meditation, and each moment of understanding, I move closer to the essence of Thoth's teachings and, perhaps, to the heart of my own soul's quest for truth.

Chapter 12: Renewing the Quest for Ancient Wisdom

As we stand at the crossroads of our understanding, the mysteries of the Emerald Tablets beckon once more. The wisdom of Thoth, captured within those ancient engravings, seems to whisper across the ages, urging us to seek the knowledge that has long been forgotten yet is eternally relevant. In a world that often prioritizes the tangible and immediate, the timeless insights held within these texts offer a clarion call to delve deeper into the mysteries of existence and the hidden potential of the human spirit.

Thoth's legacy continues to intrigue and inspire scholars, mystics, and seekers alike. His role as the divine scribe and the embodiment of wisdom exemplifies the pursuit of understanding beyond the superficial truths we are so often content with. In renewing our quest for ancient wisdom, Thoth stands not as a relic of the past but as a beacon guiding those with the courage to explore the unknown. His teachings invite us to question, to unfold the veils of ignorance, and to embrace a richer, more nuanced understanding of the cosmos and our place within it.

The journey to uncover the depths of ancient wisdom is not merely an academic endeavor; it's a transformative experience. Engaging with the Emerald Tablets and the esoteric knowledge they contain encourages us to look within and recognize the interconnectedness of all things. This introspective gaze can lead to profound personal growth, as the ancient sages believed that the wisdom of the universe also dwells within us. By seeking, we awaken the dormant knowledge within our own consciousness, nurturing an inner transformation that echoes the alchemical processes once practiced by Thoth himself.

Future explorations of these ancient texts promise to inspire a new generation of inquisitive minds. As technology and society evolve, so too does the potential to uncover previously inaccessible insights. The Emerald Tablets, with their cryptic language and multilayered meanings, serve as a reminder that there is always more to discover on the road to enlightenment. Their influence extends beyond the script carved in stone, resonating through time to touch modern spiritual practices, creating a bridge from the past to the future.

While the path may be fraught with interpretative challenges, the quest for knowledge brings us face to face with the enduring mystery of Thoth's wisdom. The process of inquiry itself becomes a crucial part of personal development. We must welcome the questions that these texts raise, seeing them not as obstacles, but as opportunities for growth. As we navigate the complexities of contemporary life, the teachings of the Emerald Tablets offer a foundation upon which to build a more meaningful existence.

In conclusion, embracing the quest for ancient wisdom invites each of us to become a seeker in our own right. It's an invitation to explore not just the boundaries of historical knowledge but also the depths of our own potential. Whether used as a tool for spiritual enhancement or as inspiration for intellectual pursuits, the Emerald Tablets and the teachings of Thoth resonate with those who dare to listen. Thus, our journey continues, and with it, the promise of renewal and enlightenment emerges anew.

Thoth's Role in the Quest for Knowledge Today

In a world saturated with information yet often devoid of wisdom, the ancient deity Thoth emerges as a beacon for those yearning for deeper truths. His essence, once interwoven with the myths and knowledge of ancient Egypt, now whispers to us as a guide in our modern pursuit of understanding. Thoth's intimate connection to the Emerald Tablets not only enriches our historical perspective but also challenges us to expand our philosophical horizons. As we renew our quest for ancient wisdom, Thoth invites us to view knowledge not as a static commodity but as an ever-evolving journey that demands both humility and courage.

Why does Thoth resonate so powerfully today? Perhaps it's his embodiment of the eternal scribe, the patron of scholars and seekers alike. In the chaotic symphony of modern life, Thoth provides a nuanced perspective on balance, urging us to weigh logic alongside intuition. For the seeker, this is more than theoretical exercise—it's an approach to life itself. By harmonizing the analytical with the mystical, Thoth teaches us to explore both the seen and unseen worlds with equal fervor.

Moreover, Thoth's role today transcends mere knowledge acquisition. His wisdom encompasses the transformative process that knowledge brings. In a digital age rich with instant information, the art of transformation is often overlooked. Yet, through such transformation, Thoth fosters a profound metamorphosis within the seeker. The journey of deciphering the Emerald Tablets becomes an allegory for personal growth, where each insight reveals a layer of ourselves previously uncharted.

As we delve deeper into this quest, Thoth's teachings reveal their adaptability. His principles serve as a framework for examining today's existential questions. How do we navigate a world increasingly dominated by technology? How do we cultivate ethical wisdom in the face of rapid change? Through Thoth, these ancient conundrums transform into relevant guideposts. His wisdom advises us to embrace the duality of knowledge—understanding that wisdom doesn't just expand outwardly but also inwardly.

The resurgence of interest in Thoth and the Emerald Tablets signals a collective longing for authenticity and enduring truths. This revival isn't merely about resurrecting old beliefs but integrating them into the current zeitgeist. By doing so, Thoth enriches our spiritual discourse and anchors us as we explore new frontiers of consciousness. Thus, he assumes an indispensable role in our current quest, offering clarity amid confusion and a timeless compass to navigate the vicissitudes of modern life.

In closing, Thoth's enduring influence reflects the inherent human desire for holistic understanding—a synthesis of ancient wisdom with contemporary inquiry. As we stand on the threshold of this renewed exploration, Thoth beckons us to venture beyond superficial knowledge, urging a profound engagement with the mysteries of existence. Through this ancient guide, the quest for knowledge becomes not just a pursuit but a journey of the soul, awakening us to the infinite potential dwelling within.

Inspiring Future Explorations of Ancient Texts reveals an enticing horizon for seekers, compelling them to ponder the untouched landscapes of ancient wisdom. We've navigated through Thoth's ageless quest for knowledge, understanding how his timeless teachings resonate with contemporary seekers eager to unearth meaning. Now, let's shift our focus to how this quest revitalizes our pursuit of ancient texts, sparking new investigations of these intricate and often ambiguous writings.

The allure of ancient texts lies in their enigmatic nature, presenting riddles wrapped in layers of metaphor and symbolism. They're not just relics of the past but vibrantly alive, speaking to us in whispers waiting to be unraveled. As we deepen our engagement with Thoth's teachings, we find touches of this same energy compelling us to seek out and explore texts from diverse traditions. It's an invitation to dive into a sea of ancient wisdom, where understanding is a quest, not a destination.

Crucially, Thoth's role in the quest for knowledge today is as a catalyst for this continued exploration. His symbolic importance and the mysteries enshrined in texts like the Emerald Tablets spur the imagination, urging scholars and mystics alike to analyze, interpret, and re-interpret these age-old writings. The process of deciphering them becomes a transformative journey, perpetually renewing our connection to the ancients.

We live in an era where information is prolific, yet true wisdom remains rare. Though we have tools undreamt of by past scholars, there is often a gap between access and understanding. Thoth's teachings offer a bridge. They not only remind us of the depth contained within these ancient documents but also urge us to view them through lenses that mix intuition and scholarly rigor. This is where future explorations gain potency; they are not just archaeological or academic pursuits but deeply personal journeys evolving with each reader who embarks on them.

The future exploration of ancient texts doesn't belong solely to historians or archaeologists. The simplicity and interconnectedness inherent in Thoth's principles appeal widely, opening the doors to many seekers from different backgrounds. Online communities and virtual study groups burgeon, uniting those with diverse perspectives who are equally passionate about uncovering the heart of these writings. Through shared discussions, interpretations multiply, enriching our understanding and igniting the spark for further inquiry across the globe.

In quiet study rooms or bustling digital spaces, the modern seeker might find themselves engrossed in technical translations or metaphysical interpretations, guiding them toward unorthodox insights. The aspirants of today don't just revisit these timeworn documents; they reanimate them, allowing them to inform present intentions and shape future aspirations. Each text becomes a canvas, offering countless shades and textures that reflect the diversity of thought inherent in human nature.

Importantly, this movement toward renewed exploration of ancient texts embodies more than just intellectual pursuit. It's an acknowledgment of humanity's endless curiosity and an homage to our ancestor's quests for truth. In embracing Thoth's role as a guide, modern seekers can embark on a path that is at once individual and collective. They will find themselves connecting ancient insights with the complexities of modern life, discovering not answers fixed in time but rather questions that challenge and expand their consciousness.

In the multidimensional tapestry of ancient wisdom, every reading, every interpretation, is an opportunity to see beyond the past into the potential of today's world. By engaging with these timeless texts, seekers are not just preserving knowledge; they're participating in a dynamic, ongoing dialogue that invigorates the spirit. The promise of future exploration lies in this vibrant synergy between past writings and contemporary seekers—a kind of alchemy that continuously transforms understanding into wisdom and wisdom into action.

As one page leads to another, as Thoth's whispers echo through the corridors of history, we might glimpse the contours of creation and mastery that these texts aspire to convey. Whether through scholarly research or personal meditation, this search for knowledge becomes a light, guiding us through the labyrinthine corridors of the unknown. By honoring this path, we find ourselves not just rooting through ancient sands for nuggets of wisdom but joining a conversation as old as the stars, eager to pass it on to future generations.

The quest to uncover the wisdom embedded in ancient texts and to align it with modern insights represents both a challenge and an aspiration. The seekers who follow Thoth's enduring legacy in their exploration know that there is much more hidden beneath the visible layers. It's the possibility of this hidden dimension that makes the journey not only irresistible but essential, inspiring us to delve deeper, always seeking with both heart and mind.

Thus, as Thoth once carried the promise of wisdom to the ancients, his legacy continues to inspire future explorations of ancient texts, forging a bridge from the past to a future filled with potential discovery. This pursuit is not one of finding static truths but of weaving the stirring threads of human thought into an ever-expanding tapestry of awareness. The Ancient Eternal awaits, patient and full of promise, for those bold enough to embrace its call.

The Continuing Influence on Personal Growth

In the ever-evolving journey of self-discovery and personal growth, the teachings of the Emerald Tablets offer a timeless beacon, guiding seekers toward deeper understanding. These ancient texts, steeped in mystery and wisdom, have transcended time and continue to influence the path of those eager to unlock their fullest potential. As modern life grows increasingly complex, individuals look to the past, to the writings attributed to Thoth, for clarity and direction. The enduring relevance of these teachings is a testament to their profound impact on human consciousness and development.

Personal growth is not merely an isolated pursuit; it's a tapestry woven through experiences, knowledge, and transformation. Thoth's teachings encourage seekers to delve within, urging the exploration of the self in relation to the universe. This inward journey is mirrored in the Hermetic principle, "As above, so below," highlighting the unity between the macrocosm and the microcosm. By understanding the interconnectedness of all things, individuals can gain insights into their own existence and purpose.

The tablets' influence on personal growth is evident in their promotion of self-reflection and introspection. In a world often focused on external achievements, these ancient texts emphasize the importance of inner cultivation. Through contemplation and meditation, practitioners can align their inner worlds with the universal truths espoused by Thoth, fostering a symbiotic relationship that nurtures both personal and spiritual development.

Moreover, Thoth's wisdom advocates for the development of virtues such as patience, resilience, and compassion. These principles, though simple in form, serve as cornerstones in the quest for self-improvement and enlightenment. The Emerald Tablets inspire individuals to embody these virtues, transforming not only themselves but also their interactions with others—essentially contributing to a ripple effect of growth within their communities.

A key aspect of the tablets' teachings is the notion of transformation, a concept deeply rooted in alchemical traditions. Personal growth is the modern-day alchemical process where individuals transmute their base selves into higher, refined beings. The cyclical nature of growth mirrors the alchemical cycle of calcination, dissolution, and eventual purification, guiding seekers through the challenges and breakthroughs necessary for profound change.

In this transformative process, the Emerald Tablets serve not just as texts but as catalytic touchstones. They provoke thought, inspire change, and often unsettle existing beliefs, pushing seekers to step beyond their comfort zones. This disturbance is crucial for personal growth, as it often precedes breakthroughs and new understandings, laying the foundation for the emergence of a more conscious and aligned self.

The influence of these ancient teachings extends into modern spiritual practices, where rituals and meditations are informed by Thoth's wisdom. By incorporating these elements, practitioners create an environment conducive to personal growth, blending the sacred with the mundane to forge a path toward enlightenment.

The continuing relevance of these teachings can also be seen in their adaptability to contemporary life. As modern seekers interpret the tablets through the lens of current experiences and challenges, they find that the core messages remain steadfast. This adaptability allows for a renewed quest for knowledge, encouraging individuals to develop a personal philosophy that resonates with the essence of the ancient wisdom they seek.

Throughout time, the teachings of the Emerald Tablets have provided invaluable insights into human nature and the potential for growth. By integrating these principles, seekers can navigate the complexities of the modern world with a mindset rooted in ancient wisdom. This synthesis of past and present elevates personal growth beyond mere self-improvement, transforming it into a holistic journey toward a harmonious existence with oneself and the universe.

In conclusion, the enduring influence of the Emerald Tablets on personal growth continues to inspire and guide individuals on their quest for inner realization. By embracing the principles of Thoth, seekers can unlock the infinite potential within, forever altering their trajectory and leaving an indelible mark on the tapestry of human consciousness.

Conclusion

In retracing the journey through the esoteric realm of the Emerald Tablets, it becomes evident that these ancient texts are more than mere artifacts of the distant past. They offer profound insights into the human condition, touching upon themes that transcend time and space. The teachings attributed to Thoth encapsulate a wisdom that speaks not only to the intellect but also to the soul. It is this duality that has captured the imagination of seekers throughout the ages, prompting them to delve deeper into the mysteries of existence.

The vibrant tapestry woven by the Tablets is rich with allegories and metaphors, each thread revealing layers of meaning waiting to be unraveled. The principles espoused within these texts have trickled down through the annals of history, finding renewed relevance in the modern age. As contemporary spiritual movements look towards the past for guidance, the tablets serve as a bridge between ancient wisdom and current thought, offering clarity in a world often shrouded in complexity.

One cannot ignore the impact the Emerald Tablets have had on diverse philosophical and spiritual disciplines, such as alchemy and hermeticism. These traditions, rooted in introspective thought and transformative practices, draw heavily from the teachings said to be channeled by Thoth. Indeed, the notions of transformation and enlightenment continue to resonate with those who traverse the labyrinthine paths of self-discovery.

Importantly, the Tablets invite an exploration of consciousness, urging individuals to look beyond the surface and into the deeper currents of reality. This exploration acts as a catalyst for personal growth, encouraging introspection and the shedding of ignorance. As seekers of truth engage with the Tablets, they are compelled to reconcile the paradoxes and wisdom within, ultimately leading to a harmonious integration of mind, body, and spirit.

While the historical and cultural origins of the Emerald Tablets remain shrouded in mystery, this enigmatic nature only adds to their allure. The ongoing scholarly debates and interpretations highlight the dynamic relationship between the text and its varied readers, each bringing their perspective into the engagement. These dialogues are crucial, as they keep the wisdom of the Tablets alive, allowing them to evolve and adapt across generations.

The journey with the Emerald Tablets is akin to a pilgrimage, not to a holy land, but to the sacred confines of the self. They challenge us to question the known and embrace the unknown, beckoning us to embark on a quest for knowledge that is both ancient and ever-renewing. Thoth's role as a guide in this quest underscores the timeless quest for wisdom that transcends cultural and temporal boundaries.

As we conclude our exploration, it is clear that the influence of the Emerald Tablets reaches far beyond doctrinal or cultural constraints. They represent an intrinsic drive towards understanding and unity, offering insights that resonate with our shared humanity. The secrets they hold are not withheld but are invitations for a personal revelation and transformation, each reader deciphering meaning through their own lens.

Thus, in embracing the wisdom of the Emerald Tablets, we renew our commitment to seek truth, grow in understanding, and contribute positively to the ever-spiraling journey of human consciousness. As they continue to inspire and guide, the Tablets remain a living testimony to the power of ancient knowledge, forever relevant in kindling the flame of wisdom for future generations eager to uncover the mysteries of existence.

Appendix A: Appendix

In our journey through the mystique of the Emerald Tablets, the appendix offers a gateway to further exploration and invites seekers to delve deeper into the arcane realms that lie beyond the scope of this book. Here, we provide additional resources meticulously curated to enhance your understanding and foster a personal connection with the ancient wisdom encapsulated in the tablets. This section serves as a bridge linking the cryptic teachings of Thoth with contemporary scholarship, esoteric communities, and the evolving interpretations that continuously reshape our perception of these mystical relics. As you peruse these resources, you'll find pathways leading to enriched insights, evoking the spirit of inquiry that drives humankind to explore not only the outer cosmos but the hidden chambers within the self. Whether you're drawn to academic discussions or the transformative practices rooted in Thoth's teachings, these resources offer a myriad of avenues for expanding both knowledge and spirit.

Additional Resources for Further Study

For those who feel the siren call to dig deeper into the enigmatic teachings of the Emerald Tablets, a treasure trove of resources awaits your exploration. The journey into ancient wisdom doesn't end with this book; it beckons you to tread further paths, each promising revelations as profound as those you've encountered thus far. In a world increasingly intrigued by the metaphysical and the esoteric, the thirst for knowledge is quenched not by singular sources but by a confluence of perspectives that illuminate and deepen one's understanding.

Books remain one of the most accessible ways to delve into the depths of Thoth's wisdom. Numerous authors have tackled the subject, each bringing their unique flair to interpretations of these ancient texts. Consider exploring translations and commentaries by scholars such as Isaac Newton and Helena Blavatsky, who have applied their scholarly rigor and mystical insight to interpret the Tablets. Their works offer diverse angles and can help you understand how ancient wisdom has shaped philosophical thought throughout history.

In addition, the writings of contemporary authors on alchemy and Hermetic philosophy provide valuable insights into how these age-old principles remain relevant today. Authors like Manly P. Hall and Carl Gustav Jung offer interpretations that bridge ancient metaphors with modern psychology, opening new doors to understanding the human psyche and its connection to universal truths. Engaging with contemporary interpretations can offer fresh perspectives on how the teachings of the Tablets can apply to today's world and your personal journey.

Digital platforms offer a modern avenue for exploration, filled with forums and online communities dedicated to the discussion and study of the Emerald Tablets. Websites, webinars, and online courses hosted by experts and enthusiasts alike can provide interactive and engaging ways to connect with like-minded seekers. Consider joining these communities to participate in discussions, ask questions, and share insights, all while learning from others' experiences and interpretations.

Furthermore, academic journals offer rigorous examinations of the historical, cultural, and linguistic aspects of the Emerald Tablets. These publications often feature articles that delve into the archaeological context of the Tablets, analyze the nuances of their language, and explore their influence on various spiritual traditions. By engaging with these scholarly works, you can appreciate the depth of research and analysis that continues to inform our understanding of the Tablets.

The realm of audiovisual media also presents an array of documentaries and lectures available through streaming services or educational platforms. These resources can provide visual and narrative experiences that bring the mystical narratives to life. Seek out documentaries that focus on ancient Egyptian culture, the life of Thoth, and the impact of Hermetic philosophy throughout history. These visual explorations can help reinforce and expand upon the textual insights you've acquired.

For the more introspective traveler, embarking on guided meditative practices and rituals inspired by the teachings of the Emerald Tablets can be profoundly enlightening. Many spiritual retreats and workshops offer experiences rooted in ancient wisdom where you can learn techniques to unlock inner truths and harness your own mystical powers, whether through meditation, visualization, or energy work. These practices provide a direct experiential connection to the teachings, offering a path to embody knowledge rather than just understand it intellectually.

In particular, look for traditional ceremonies that incorporate elements of Hermeticism and alchemy, as these often reference principles found within the Emerald Tablets. Whether it's a solitary practice or in a community setting, these experiences can deepen your personal connection to the teachings, allowing for transformative personal insight that aligns with the essence of Thoth's wisdom.

Lastly, for those intent on a more immersive experience, consider exploring study groups or joining societies dedicated to the exploration of Hermetic teachings. Such groups frequently meet to discuss texts, share personal insights, and engage in collective learning endeavors. They provide not only a collaborative learning atmosphere but also foster a sense of community among fellow seekers of wisdom.

The journey to unveil ancient wisdom is never truly complete, for each source, experience, and discussion offers potential revelations. By drawing on these additional resources, you open yourself to a continuous path of discovery, where the echoes of ancient teachings can inform and enrich the tapestry of contemporary life. As you delve into these layers of knowledge, ancient and modern, profound mysteries of the universe may gradually unfold before you, affirming the timeless relevance of the Emerald Tablets and their enduring legacy. Happy exploring, and may your pursuit of wisdom be ever fruitful and enlightening.

Glossary of Key Terms and Concepts

In this section, you'll find essential terms and concepts that form the bedrock of the mystical teachings within the Emerald Tablets, providing a foundation for your journey into ancient wisdom. These terms bridge the arcane with the modern, helping seekers get to the heart of Thoth's timeless insights.

- **Alchemy:** More than the medieval pursuit of turning base metals into gold, alchemy is a spiritual discipline aimed at personal transformation and achieving enlightenment, deeply rooted in the teachings of the Tablets.
- **Correspondence Principle:** A core hermetic axiom suggesting a mirroring between different planes of existence, captured in the phrase "as above, so below," illustrating the universe's interconnected nature.
- **Emerald Tablets:** An enigmatic collection of writings attributed to Thoth, said to contain secrets of the universe, consciousness, and the path to spiritual enlightenment.
- **Hermeticism:** A philosophical and spiritual tradition based on the teachings of Hermes Trismegistus, entwined with the lessons of the Emerald Tablets, offering insights into the nature of reality, divinity, and the human soul.
- **Meditation Practices:** Techniques derived from Thoth's teachings, focusing on inner stillness and awakening higher consciousness to access the deeper truths hidden within oneself.
- **Mythology of Thoth:** The rich tapestry of myths surrounding Thoth, revered as the god of wisdom, writing, and magic in ancient Egyptian culture, providing a backdrop for the lessons enshrined in the Tablets.
- **Symbolism and Metaphors:** The language of the Tablets is

143

rife with symbolism and metaphors, inviting readers to uncover hidden meanings and deeper truths beyond the literal interpretation.

- **Transmutation:** A central concept in alchemy, this refers to both the physical and spiritual transformation, emphasizing the inner journey from the mundane to the divine as outlined in Thoth's teachings.

- **Thoth:** An ancient Egyptian deity, often depicted as a man with the head of an ibis or a baboon, considered the architect of writing, magic, and wisdom, and the narrator of the Emerald Tablets.

- **Wisdom Schools:** Ancient centers of learning inspired by Thoth, where initiates studied the mysteries of spirituality, the universe, and the self, laying the groundwork for esoteric traditions.

Understanding these terms will serve as your compass, guiding you through the intricate labyrinth of thoughts, symbols, and teachings brought forth by the Emerald Tablets. As these ancient concepts unfold, they promise to illuminate the paths towards both personal transformation and a deeper comprehension of the cosmos.

Don't miss out!

Visit the website below and you can sign up to receive emails whenever david holman publishes a new book. There's no charge and no obligation.

https://books2read.com/r/B-A-STXT-GDYIF

BOOKS 2 READ

Connecting independent readers to independent writers.

Did you love *Echoes Of Eternity; Unlocking Thoths Mysteries*? Then you should read *Applying The Principles Of The Universal Laws*[1] by david holman!

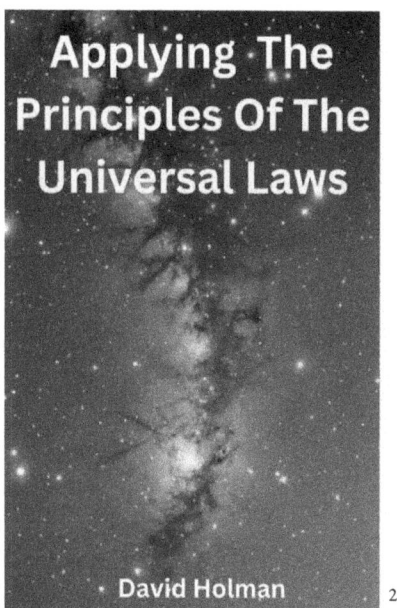

In a world where we constantly seek meaning, success, and happiness, understanding the fundamental principles that govern our reality can be transformative. "Applying the Principles of the Universal Laws" is an illuminating journey through the core laws of the universe, designed to empower you with the knowledge and tools to create the life you desire. This book is not just about understanding these laws but about applying them practically to manifest profound changes in your life.

This book delves into the ten most powerful universal laws: the Law of Attraction, Law of Vibration, Law of Action, Law of Cause and Effect, Law of Correspondence, Law of Polarity, Law of Rhythm, Law

1. https://books2read.com/u/bMl1qk

2. https://books2read.com/u/bMl1qk

of Relativity, Law of Gender, and the Law of Perpetual Transmutation of Energy. Each chapter provides an in-depth exploration of these laws, followed by practical steps, techniques, and guidance on how to apply them effectively.

Key Takeaways

Self-Awareness and Reflection

Understanding your inner world and how it affects your external reality is the foundation of transformation. Regular self-reflection, mindfulness, and journaling are essential practices for gaining self-awareness.

Positive Mindset

Cultivating a positive mindset is crucial for aligning with your desires. Techniques such as positive affirmations, gratitude practices, and reframing negative thoughts help maintain a constructive outlook.

Intentional Actions

Purposeful and consistent actions are necessary to manifest your goals. Setting clear intentions, developing actionable plans, and prioritizing tasks ensure that your actions lead to desired outcomes.

Balancing Energies

Recognizing and balancing both masculine and feminine energies within yourself leads to a harmonious life. Engaging in creative expression and structured planning supports this balance.

Adaptability and Resilience

Being flexible and open to change is essential for navigating life's challenges. Developing resilience and viewing setbacks as opportunities for growth help you stay on course.

Holistic Approach

Maintaining a holistic approach that balances action with rest, and mental focus with physical well-being, ensures overall harmony and balance. Incorporating self-care practices into your daily routine supports your well-being.

Continuous Learning

Lifelong learning and continuous improvement are key to personal growth. Seeking feedback, embracing new experiences, and staying open to learning enhance your journey of transformation.

Final Thoughts

"Applying the Principles of the Universal Laws" is more than just a book—it's a comprehensive guide to creating a life of purpose, success, and fulfillment. By understanding and applying the universal laws, you can unlock your potential and manifest your dreams. This book provides the knowledge, tools, and techniques you need to navigate your journey of self-discovery and personal growth.

Whether you're new to the concept of universal laws or looking to deepen your understanding, this book offers valuable insights and practical steps to help you harness these powerful principles. Remember, the journey of transformation is ongoing. Stay dedicated, remain positive, and trust in the process. The universe is ready to respond to your thoughts, actions, and energy—use these laws wisely to create the life you envision.

Also by david holman

Riot Survival Guide
Guide To Natural Disasters
ElectroCulture Basics
The Taylor Swift Effect
Athletic Training
Beginners Guide To YOGA
Functional Fitness
Meditation Basics
Surviving Catastrophe In an Urban Enviroment
Urban Gardening Tips And Tricks For Beginners
Applying The Principles Of The Universal Laws
Surviving The Rising Cost Of Everything
Rescue In The Woods
Bruce Lee's Way: The Art Of A Modern Day Warrior
Slayers Creed
The Path Of Jeet Kune Do
How To Be Your Own Doctor
Muscles And Strength Building
Legacy of Preparedness
Chaos To Calm
Life Of Contentment
Streams Of Prosperity
Path Of The Warrior
Unleash The Dragon:Mastering Jeet Kune Do For Life.
Echoes Of Eternity; Unlocking Thoths Mysteries

The Art Of Alignment :Crafting your Inner and Outer Mastery

Milton Keynes UK
Ingram Content Group UK Ltd.
UKHW030145051224
452010UK00001B/128

9 798230 854302